THE LEGAL SYSTEM OF LOUISIANA

STATE OF LOUISIANA
UNION • JUSTICE
• CONFIDENCE •

Bibliothèque de l'Association
Henri Capitant

*Library of the Association
Henri Capitant*

LEGAL SYSTEMS SERIES

THE LEGAL SYSTEM OF LOUISIANA

EDITORS

Alain A. Levasseur
Professor of Law Emeritus, LSU

J. Randall Trahan
Professor of Law, LSU

David Gruning
Professor of Law, Loyola New Orleans

Carolina Academic Press
Durham, North Carolina

Association
Henri Capitant

LGDJ une marque de Lextenso

ISBN: 978-1-5310-1423-0
eISBN: 978-1-5310-1424-7

Carolina Academic Press, LLC
700 Kent Street
Durham, North Carolina 27701
Telephone (919) 489-7486
Fax (919) 493-5668
www.cap-press.com

Printed in the United States of America

THE SERIES

For over eighty years now, the Association Henri Capitant has endeavored to spread, update and promote the law of the European continent. Traditionally, it has done so with holding yearly international and national *Journées* (conferences), as well as other multilateral and bilateral meetings.

The many national Sections or Chapters of the Association have been urged to present, in concise books, the high points of their legal system. Though these books were originally written in French, they are now being translated into English so that they will be accessible to English-speaking audiences.

All the books translated into English follow the original French text as well as a standard format. In this way, the books expose the reader to the fundamental features and foundations of a variety of legal systems that make up what has become known as "continental law."

In all English versions of the books, the editors have attempted to use, where appropriate, the same civil or continental law terminology, and to adopt as simple and straightforward an English language as possible. In other words, these books are meant to make accessible the legal systems of continental law countries, states or provinces to as large a readership as possible.

The guiding purpose behind this Series is to present a comparative law survey of a variety of legal systems in such a way that the reader will be able to cross the confining frontiers of his own legal system to better understand it and to find in other legal systems reasons and grounds to modify and, possibly, to improve its own legal system.

[*Editors' note*: every book written in French is translated in the country of origin, be it in the Netherlands, Romania, France . . . . The Editors' task is to bring cohesion and uniformity to the English texts submitted to them.]

Denis Mazeaud
Professeur, Université Panthéon-Assas (Paris II)

Philippe Dupichot
Professeur, Université Panthéon-Sorbonne (Paris I)

Cyril Grimaldi
Professeur, Université Paris XIII

Alain Levasseur
Professor, LSU Law School

Randall Trahan
Professor, LSU Law School

David Gruning
Professor, Loyola Law School

CHAPTER AUTHORS

John Church
Professor of Law, Louisiana State University
Delictual Liability (Torts)

William Corbett
Professor of Law, Louisiana State University
Labor and Employment Law

David Gruning
Professor of Law, Loyola University
Constitutional Framework, The Family

Wendell Holmes
Professor of Law, Louisiana State University
Louisiana Business Entities

Alain Levasseur
Professor of Law, Emeritus, Louisiana State University
Sources of Law, Legal Actors, Contract, Quasi-Contracts, Criminal Law

Agustin Parise
Assistant Professor of Law, Maastricht University
Legal History

« THE AUTHORS »

Randall Trahan
Professor of Law, Louisiana State University
Sources of Law, Property

Sandi Varnado
Associate Professor of Law, Loyola University
Persons

TABLE OF CONTENTS

THE LEGAL SYSTEM OF LOUISIANA

CHAPTER ONE

LEGAL HISTORY

The state of Louisiana is rich in its social and legal history, especially, the legal history of its private law. Louisiana has traditionally been considered to be a member of the continental European system or civil law tradition. It is the only state in the United States with codes that originally followed the tenets of nineteenth-century continental European codes.

Early in its history, the present-day territory of Louisiana was inhabited by a diversity of Native American groups. Then, Spaniards were the first Europeans to explore the region. In 1528, Pánfilo de Narváez reached the mouth of the Mississippi River. Later, in 1539, the Governor of Cuba, Hernando de Soto, sailed to Florida and explored the region. He crossed the northern part of the current states of Louisiana and Arkansas, and then sailed on the Mississippi River towards the Gulf of Mexico.

France expanded its presence in the Americas during the following century. In 1682, René Robert Cavelier, sieur de La Salle, took possession of the lower region of the Mississippi River and named it *Louisiane* in honor of the French King Louis XIV. The French monarch signed a Royal Charter in 1712 in favor of Antoine Crozat, a wealthy merchant, by which the French ordinances and edicts, together with the customs and usages of Paris, were to become the law of the territory.

France ceded Louisiana to Spain as a result of the Treaty of Fontainebleau (1762) followed by the Treaty of Paris of 1763. Seven years later, in 1769, the Spanish Governor Alejandro O'Reilly implemented the Spanish Colonial system of government and replaced the then existing French laws (e.g., *Coutume de Paris*) with the Spanish laws. He instructed—on November 25, 1769—the manner of instituting suits, civil and criminal, and of pronouncing judgments in general, in conformity to the laws of Spain. From that time on, Spanish law became the law of the land.

Napoléon Bonaparte negotiated the return of Louisiana to France with the Treaty of San Ildefonso (1800). The territory covered most of the current central part of the United States. During that second French period, the applicable law was still Spanish and no significant changes were made to the jurisprudence of the region. This is attested in the correspondence between Pierre Clément de Laussat (French Prefect in Louisiana) and Denis Decrès (French Ministry of the Navy). Further, it should be noted that the Northern parishes of current Louisiana remained under Spanish control until 1810.

Louisiana would live briefly under French domain until the Treaty of Paris (1803) was signed resulting in the "Louisiana Purchase." The first proclamation of William C. Claiborne, then Commissioner, was to preserve the laws that applied at the time of the Purchase (i.e., Spanish laws and the French *Code noir*). Later, an act of the US Congress dated March 26, 1804, established that "the laws in force in the said territory, at the commencement of this act, and not inconsistent with the provisions thereof, shall continue in force, until altered, modified, or repealed by the legislature." The continued existence of Spanish laws was reaffirmed by an act of the US Congress dated March 5, 1805. In 1812, Louisiana became a "state" and was admitted as the eighteenth state of the Union.

The first Louisiana Constitution was approved by the US Congress in 1812, and it resulted from the work of a Constitutional Convention presided by Julien Poydras. That first Louisiana Constitution would then be modified on numerous occasions (*i.e.*, 1845, 1852, 1861, 1864, 1868, 1879, 1898, 1913, 1921, 1974). Language is especially relevant for the understanding of the process of codification in Louisiana. The first Louisiana Constitution stated that the laws be enacted in the language of the US Constitution. In 1845 the Louisiana Constitution required that all official promulgated texts be in French and English. In 1868 the Louisiana Constitution returned to mandatory promulgation in the English language.

Louisiana was no exception to the nineteenth-century codification movement that spread throughout the Western hemisphere. The legal culture of Louisiana was an isolated civil law island partially surrounded by a sea of common law, a unique status that had to be safeguarded in order to survive. Thus, codification endeavors in Louisiana started immediately after the Louisiana Purchase, and reflected an oscillation between the adoption of the continental European and the common law systems. The first generation of codes was drafted during the first quarter of the nineteenth century.

The first decisions on the adoption of provisions from different systems were taken in criminal law and criminal procedure. An Act for the Punishment of Crimes and Misdemeanors (Punishment Act, 1805) was adopted and in 52 articles, written both in French and English, the text regulated crimes, punishments, and procedure. In 1824, Edward Livingston, a common law trained lawyer from New York, formulated his system of criminal law, comprising a book of definitions and four codes: crimes and punishments, procedure, evidence, and reform and prison discipline. The works of Livingston on criminal law were never enacted in Louisiana, though his system of penal law developed into a major source for criminal law codification around the World particularly in South America with the Brazilian criminal code (1830) as an example. Codification of criminal procedure took place in Louisiana in 1928, whereas codification of criminal law was delayed until 1942. The criminal law of Louisiana followed to a great extent common law principles while the continental European system was neglected.

Changes in civil procedure were also tackled early during the territorial period. The Spanish period had been marked by ordinances and instructions issued by O'Reilly that mainly regulated practice and procedure in the region, together with some French practices that persisted. Early accounts show confusion before the courts of law on account of the fact that judges were trained in different systems and claims were filed in different languages. An Act of 22 articles Regulating the Practice of the Superior Court in Civil Causes (Practice Act, 1805) was elaborated, mainly by Livingston and written both in French and English. The Practice Act, supplemented by a second Act of that same year. These Acts were very succinct and were silent in several areas. This created so much uncertainty that the legislature appointed Louis Moreau-Lislet, Pierre Derbigny and Edward Livingston to elaborate a Code of Practice in Civil Cases for the State of Louisiana (Practice Code, 1825). The text, adopted both in French and English, comprised 1,161 articles, being divided into two parts. This Practice Code reflected a combination of continental European and common law principles. It remained in effect until 1870.

In the area of civil law the erection of a defensive system against the common law manifested itself early with the controlling influence of continental European ideas. The months of May and June of 1806 were marked by events that reflected the profound interest of local inhabitants for the continental European system in private law matters. In May 1806 the local legislative Assembly adopted an Act that stated very explicitly that the pre-existing Spanish and Roman laws were to govern the territory. However Governor Claiborne vetoed that Act. The New Orleans newspaper, Le Telegraphe, published a very poignant "Manifesto" dated May 28 that was signed by members of the House of Representatives. They protested vehemently against Claiborne's veto, proposed the dissolution of the legislature and explained the reasons why they preferred the continental European system over the common law system. In June, James Brown and Moreau-Lislet were appointed to draft a "Civil Code." Their work resulted in the "Digest of the Civil Laws now in Force in the Territory of Orleans" (Digest of 1808). The Digest comprised 2,160 articles and was divided into a "Preliminary Title" and three "Books." That text, which was adopted by the local legislature, was drafted in French and thereafer translated into English. It did not include an "exposé des motifs." A copy of the Digest of 1808, the "de la Vergne manuscript" includes references, referred to as "Sources," to Roman and Spanish materials, together with references to French texts of Roman grounding (e.g., Robert Joseph Pothier, Jean Domat). In 1971, Professor Rodolfo Batiza (Tulane) concluded that approximately 85% of the text of the Digest of 1808 was actually made of "words" extracted from French texts. In contrast, Professors Robert A. Pascal and Alain Levasseur (LSU) explained that the drafters of the Digest had merely used the texts available to them in the French language because they actually reflected the substance of the Spanish and Roman sources of law they had been instructed to take into account. Since French law, made up of many elements of Roman law and Romanized texts, and Spanish law also derived from Roman or Roman-Visigothic sources of law were, in substance, very much alike, the use of the French language from "French texts" was only a natural and expeditious vehicle to reflect the same "substantive law" expressed elsewhere in the Spanish language and in Latin.

Codification of the civil law of Louisiana did not stop with the enactment of the Digest of 1808. Derbigny, Livingston, and Moreau-Lislet drafted a new text of 3,522 articles which was adopted in 1825 by the local legislature under the title of "Civil Code of the State of Louisiana" (Civil Code, 1825). The structure of the Civil Code was similar to that of the Digest of 1808 but it was more detailed as it included 3522 articles. Written in French and then translated in English, this Code of 1825 is still considered as the basic "Civil Code of Louisiana."

The codification process of the civil law continued in Louisiana well into the rest of the nineteenth century and during the twentieth century. A major revision was undertaken successfully in 1870 while a second revision effort failed in 1908. The Louisiana State Law Institute (LSLI) has been undertaking a series of revisions since the 1970s. As regards the civil law and the civil Code in particular, Louisiana does follow the models and principles coming from the continental European systems.

The Spanish Ordinances of Bilbao (1737) had been applied in Louisiana when dealing with commercial matters. However, the effects of the Louisiana Purchase and the commercial needs reflected that some inhabitants also valued other legal documents pertaining commerce. Accordingly, the local legislature adopted the previously mentioned Act (1806) in which they stated which laws would govern the territory. That Act stated that the Ordinances of Bilbao had full authority in the territory and that Roman, English, French and US sources could be also used in commercial matters. Moreau-Lislet, Derbigny, and Livingston completed a draft of a commercial code (Commercial Code) by 1825, though it was never adopted by the local legislature. The Commercial Code had 1,963 articles, it was divided into two books, and was drafted in French and English. The Commercial Code used the French *Code de commerce* as a model, though it included several original provisions. The commercial provisions of other US states slowly started to percolate into the law of Louisiana. In commercial law, local inhabitants seemed to prefer the flexibility that their practices provided.

The Louisiana legal system went through some hard times in its attempt to remain within the civil law tradition. In 1937, Professor Gordon Ireland (LSU) expressed the view that Louisiana had become a common law state, that opinions from the courts had become precedents and that the Code was only a compilation of courts decisions. Dean Hébert (LSU), and other colleagues, refuted Ireland's statements in the "Great Debate" to state unequivocally that Louisiana belonged to the civil law tradition. This "Debate" prompted a strong movement for the enhancement of the civil law tradition in Louisiana under the form of revisions in and innovations of the civil Code.

LSLI is the official advisory law revision commission, law reform agency, and legal research agency for the state of Louisiana. The LSLI gained recognition through its on-going reform of the Civil Code and other equally important works. For example, the LSLI has been involved in the elaboration of the Criminal Code (1942), Louisiana Revised Statutes (1950), Code of Civil Procedure

(1960), Trust Code (1964), Code of Criminal Procedure (1966), Mineral Code (1974), and Children's Code (1991). The LSLI has also been involved in the translation of doctrinal French works into English (e.g., Charles Aubry and Charles Rau, François Gény, Marcel Planiol) since the early years, and these works are often referred to by courts of law.

Louisiana, as mentioned before, never enacted a commercial code whereas the other states of the United States adopted the Uniform Commercial Code (UCC). Louisiana is, therefore, surrounded by the UCC and claims for its adoption from common-law trained lawyers have been forcefully expressed. As a result, the adoption of some Titles of the UCC has been gradual in Louisiana in the last 35 years. However there are major areas of resistance to the full adoption of the UCC, particularly as regards the law of "sale," "lease," "bulk sales." Title 10 of the Louisiana Revised Statutes may be considered as the "Uniform Commercial Code." of Louisiana. Even though Articles 2 and 6 of the UCC are not applied directly in Louisiana, some of their dispositions have entered into the legal framework of the state. For example, the revision of Title 7 on Sale, Book III of the Civil Code, includes a recent Chapter 13, "Sale of Movables," which incorporates some of the ideas that exist in the UCC, such as the battle of the forms, the buyer's rights of inspection and of rejection of nonconforming goods. Preservation of civil-law principles had to be considered during the revision process of the Civil Code and during the incorporation of provisions from the UCC. It should be noted that the UN Convention on Contracts for the International Sale of Goods (1980) was likewise influential in the commercial law of Louisiana.

The legal system of the state of Louisiana, rich in history, bijuridical in its substantive law, mixed in its administration of justice, remains, in its heart and soul, a civil law jurisdiction struggling for its survival. It enjoys a unique and exemplary advantage, even an exclusive benefit little known and therefore not appreciated in the civil law world, which is that "We," in Louisiana, are the only civil law jurisdiction among all the existing civil law jurisdictions to speak, write and think the civil law in the English language (not the English of the "common law") and that since the Digest of 1808, more than two centuries ago. The English language on one side and the French and Spanish languages on the other side bind the legal system of Louisiana in a unique and singular fashion to the two main legal traditions that make up its "mixed legal system."

Bibliography

Cairns, J. W.: "The de la Vergne Volume and the Digest of 1808," *Tulane European & Civil Law Forum*, 24, 2009, p. 31–81.

Dargo, G.: *Jefferson's Louisiana: Politics and the Clash of Legal Traditions*, Cambridge, Harvard University Press, 1975.

Dart, H. P.: "The Legal Institutions of Louisiana," *Southern Law Quarterly*, 3, 1918, p. 247–280.

Kilbourne, R. H.: *A History of the Louisiana Civil Code: The Formative Years, 1803–1839*, Baton Rouge, LSU Law, 1987.

Levasseur, A. A.: *Louis Casimir Elisabeth Moreau-Lislet: Foster Father of Louisiana Civil Law*, Baton Rouge, LSU Law, 1996.

Murchison, K. M.: "The Judicial Revival of Louisiana's Civilian Tradition: A Surprising Triumph for the American Influence," *Louisiana Law Review*, 49, 1988, p. 1–37.

Palmer, V. V.: "The French Connection and the Spanish Perception: Historical Debates and Contemporary Evaluation of French Influence on Louisiana Civil Law," *Louisiana Law Review*, 63, 2003, p. 1067–1125.

Parise, A.: "Codification of the Law in Louisiana: Early Nineteenth-Century oscillation between Continental European and Common Law Systems," *Tulane European & Civil Law Forum*, 42, 2012, p. 133–164.

Tucker, J. H.: "Source Books of Louisiana Law I," *Tulane Law Review*, 6, 1931, p. 280–300.

Tucker, J. H.: "Source Books of Louisiana Law II," *Tulane Law Review*, 7, 1932, p. 82–95.

Yiannopoulos, A. N.: "The Civil Codes of Louisiana," Yiannopoulos, A. N. (ed.): *West's Louisiana Civil Code*, 1, Saint Paul, West, 2008, p. li–lxiv.

CHAPTER TWO

SOURCES OF LAW

1. SOURCES OF LAW IN GENERAL

On April 30, 1812, Louisiana became the eighteenth state of the federation of the United States. In so doing, from a juridical point of view, Louisiana submitted itself to a dual juridical system. It was composed, on the one side, of the federal law applicable to all of the states of the union and, on the other, of its own law, the civil law in particular, which distinguishes Louisiana from the other states. The sources of federal law must be examined separately from the sources of Louisiana law.

The sources of federal law are numerous and exhibit a hierarchical arrangement. Certain sources—the most important—are of a constitutional order; other sources, at a second level, derive their authority from the tradition of the common law; finally, others are of an administrative nature.

The Constitution of the Unites States of 1787 is the source of law that enjoys the most absolute authority, as the Supreme Court has often declared. The Constitution borrows much from the art of codification in its presentation and by virtue of the singular style of its writing. As a result, the letter of the Constitution and its literal interpretation, as is typical of the common law, have not been able to serve as limits on one of the major roles of the Supreme Court, which is to interpret the Constitution. The Court, going beyond the letter of the texts, reaches out to the intentions and objectives of the constitutional authors or "forefathers" of 1787 and often allows itself to employ *a pari ratione* and *a fortiori ratione* interpretations so as to give to the texts a contemporary foundation. The Supreme Court has thus been led to say that the judicial power of the United States extends to all affairs that arise under the dominion of the Constitution, its letter and its spirit.

At a degree immediately inferior to the Constitution one finds, at the same level, the legislation of Congress and treaties. According to the democratic principles that are incorporated into the Constitution, a treaty could not have an authority that is superior to that of legislation. In a case of conflict between a treaty and legislation, the preeminence of the one over the other depends on whether it took effect before or after the other. The courts apply the principle according to which the more recent must prevail over the more ancient. The very detailed character of federal legislation is explained, in part, by the fact that Congress is wary of the creative power of common law judges and, by this means, seeks to contain the liberty of these judges to make law and, in part, by the fact that federal legislators want to give an approach to the solution of contemporary problems that is practical, timely, and detailed.

The President of the United States enjoys the executive power that is given to him by Article II of the Constitution. As the chief of government, the president has the duty to see to the execution of all legislation, from which the importance of the presidential function arises. He can also issue decrees, regulations, or executive orders in the areas that are reserved to him.

After some hesitations, the common law was established, in particular after the Civil War, as a source of traditional law, inherited from the common law of England. Following the Commentaries of the great English jurist Blackstone, American authors, such as Kent and Story, assured the grip and the vitality of the common law. Although we are dealing here with federal law, the common law that is in question is neither a federal nor North America-wide common law. According to the Supreme Court, the federal courts must take into consideration the common law of each of the states of the federation (with the exception of the law of Louisiana) when they are called upon to render a judgment based on the common law of the state in question. There are some great similarities, indeed, often a total identity, between the common laws of the different states of the United States. Thus, if a federal common law exists, it is in reality a matter of a common law created by the jurisprudence of the states and taken into account by the federal courts where they have jurisdiction in the domains that borrow from the laws of the states.

The most classic method of reasoning the common law courts use is the literal interpretation of the legislative text. It is appropriate to give to the text the pure and simple meaning that the words of it give. This is the "plain meaning rule" or the rule of the clear and evident sense of the legislation.

Identified with the common law is the jurisprudential notion of "precedent," also known under its Latin form of *stare decisis*, which is a source of law in the common law. It is the case with certain decisions of the superior federal courts that they become "binding precedents," tying the inferior courts of the same jurisdiction. Other jurisprudential decisions have an authority that is only moral or relative: it's a matter of "persuasive precedents." The theory of precedent is more flexible in American law than it is in English law, even though it is founded on the same principles of equality before the law and of the stability and predictability of the law. For the Supreme Court, whether *stare decisis* is respected or whether it is set aside is a question that falls within the discretion of the court that is called upon to reevaluate the law that has been put in question. Several times the Supreme Court has refused to be absolutely tied by some of its prior decisions and it has often reversed some of its own decisions. This position of the Supreme Court can notably be explained by the fact that the federal courts, more than those of the state courts, do not hesitate to play an active role, under the cover of interpreting the Constitution, in bringing solutions to certain social, economic, and other problems, particularly within the framework of the "Bill of Rights."

Another source of federal law, one that is inexhaustible, are the numerous federal agencies, the creation of which dates from the beginning of the nineteenth century. It was especially in the 1930s, in response to the economic and social crises of this period, that these agencies became quite numerous. They have the task of transposing into practical and operational measures the directives that are given to them by the "enabling acts" of Congress. The agencies, such as the Federal Trade Commission, for example, make decisions that assume a legislative form where they act in the name of Congress. An agency can also be substituted for the executive. The Administrative Procedure Act of 1946 established a relatively strict framework for the exercise of the legislative, executive, and indeed judicial powers of these agencies. They have become extremely prolific sources of administrative law. Inasmuch as the exercise of their powers is submitted to the control of the ordinary federal courts, these courts, by virtue of this control, have a right of review over the activities of the two other branches of government, which, in some fashion, have been fused together in the heart of these agencies.

Among the secondary sources of law, one finds the "Restatements" and doctrine. The Restatements are methodical and systematic compilations or digests of the jurisprudence in the various particular areas of the law. These Restatements, such as the Restatement of the Law of Contracts, are the product of works undertaken by the American Law Institute, which is a private organization composed of legal practitioners, judges, and professors. As a private work, a Restatement enjoys an authority that depends on its intrinsic value as well as the prestige of the personality of its principal reporter.

As for doctrine, its contribution to the formation of the law is more important than that of English doctrine, but it is still less than that of doctrine in the countries with Romano-Germanic law. Published doctrinal works devote great attention to decisions of the courts and include commentaries on judgments and practical problems or cases. There are few works of juridical theory. Doctrine nevertheless plays a role in the systematization and unification of the law.

The "statutes" or "acts" adopted by Congress can be found in the "United States Code (Annotated)," either the USC or the USCA. One can also consult Westlaw. The "regulations," "rules," and "decisions" of the federal agencies appear in the "Federal Register" and the "Code of Federal Regulations" (CFR). The decisions of the federal courts, above all those of the Supreme Court, are published in the digests of the jurisprudence as well as by Westlaw.

2. SOURCES OF LAW IN LOUISIANA

The sources of Louisiana law correspond to the traditional classification of the sources of continental law: the written sources, on the one hand, and the non-written sources, on the other. Developments within the history of the law of Louisiana explain how Louisiana has become a jurisdiction of mixed law, with, on the one side, the common law, which has conquered all of what we could call the public and commercial law and, on the other side, a Civil Code that closely resembles the French Civil Code (see Chapter One, Legal History).

The written sources of Louisiana law are the state constitution and legislation adopted by the Louisiana legislature.

The current constitution was adopted in 1974. It contains, notably, an Article III on the legislative power, an Article IV on the executive power, and an Article V on the judicial power. It also contains Section 15 under Article III which provides that it would be contrary to the state constitution to adopt a code of legislation by way of a simple general reference. The common law is targeted here in a quite specific fashion in such a way that its introduction into Louisiana is forbidden.

Legislation is, after the Constitution, the principal source of law in that it benefits from superior authority. The Louisiana Civil Code provides, in its first article, that "[t]he sources of law are legislation and custom." Article 2 adds that "[l]egislation is a solemn expression of legislative will." As for Article 3, it declares that "[c]ustom results from practice repeated for a long time and generally accepted as having acquired the force of law. Custom may not abrogate legislation." But current Louisiana law offers no example of a custom that fulfills the conditions required by Article 3. As a result, legislation remains all the more the principal source of law given that custom could not abrogate legislation.

Among the different codes that exist one should cite the Civil Code, of course, but also the Code of Civil Procedure and the Criminal Code. Alongside the Civil Code, which is of particular interest to us, it is necessary to cite the legislation that, passed year by year, may concern the dispositions of the Civil Code. This legislation is published in the "Revised Statutes" (RS), in Title 9 in particular. Regulations issued by the Administration, or the executive power, also enjoy a superior authority, just like the famous "executive orders" put out by the state governor. The judicial power also adopts some "rules" that have the force of legislation, such as the "Rules of Professional Responsibility," which are rules of ethics. The courts can also issue "local" rules of procedure in matters for which the Code of Civil Procedure does not provide.

With respect to the category of non-written sources of law, Article 4 of the Civil Code states that "[w]hen no rule for a particular situation can be derived from legislation or custom, the court is bound to proceed according to equity. To decide equitably, resort is made to justice, reason, and prevailing usages." The word "equity" merits a special comment. It is necessary, in reading this word, to keep oneself from understanding it in the same sense as the word and concept "equity" that is a source of law in the common law. In Louisiana civil law, the concept of "equity" must be taken in the sense of *aequitas*, of justice found on equality of treatment, good morals, and moral and intellectual honesty. To these elements of the concept of equity, it is necessary to add "justice," "reason," and "prevailing usages," in other words, social practices that, without being obligatory, are widely followed.

Outside of the sources of law that are expressly cited in this article, it is necessary to add two sources called secondary, also called "persuasive," sources: which are jurisprudence and doctrine. To include jurisprudence among the secondary sources of law in Louisiana presents the risk of importing a principal source of the common law under the form of the theory of *stare decisis*. According to this theory, a court "says-declares" the law and, as a result, this law is imposed in the future in affairs of the same nature. Louisiana has rejected this theory and has made its own the doctrine of "*jurisprudence constante*," as the Supreme Court of Louisiana has often declared. The Louisiana courts consider that, under the conditions mentioned in Article 3 of the Civil Code, *jurisprudence constante* can be generative of custom and, as a consequence, can become the source of law mentioned in Article 1 of the Code. The notion of custom is sometimes assimilated, erroneously in our opinion, to the "usages" mentioned in Articles 4 and 2053 of the Civil Code.

The doctrine of *jurisprudence constante*, taught in the law schools and recognized by numerous court decisions, in particular the decisions of the Louisiana Supreme Court, has been subjected to critiques formulated by judges, often of the inferior courts, and by legal practitioners. According to these judges, once a court has rendered a judgment, it is extremely rare for this same court to rule in a contrary sense in the future; besides, a court has the natural (and some would say "professional"!) tendency to conform itself to jurisprudential decisions that have already been rendered and are known, especially when they emanate from superior courts. Finally, an inferior court does not like to see its judgments overturned by a superior court. According to this point of view, jurisprudence is, in fact, a source of law. Certain legal practitioners believe that it is absolutely necessary for them to be able to counsel and to advocate for their clients on the basis of the judicial decisions that are published in the digests of jurisprudence, which they regularly consult. It is no exaggeration to say that, as in the states of the common law, these practitioners attach more value to a judicial decision that interprets a legislative provision than to the legislative provision itself. One can see here, once again, the influence of North American juridical culture.

As for doctrine as an indirect and secondary source of law, in Louisiana it presents itself under the form of books, which may be treatises (relatively few in number), "Précis" on the Civil Code, textbooks or manuals, above all those designed for students, articles of doctrine published in the law reviews by law professors, and some translations of works of law, especially French works. One difficulty faced by Louisiana jurists who wish to write on Louisiana civil law, is to find an editor (with the exceptions of Carolina Academic Press and West Publishing), since the market for books of Louisiana law is limited to Louisiana, where the civil law exists, in contrast to the 49 markets the common law states represent. Despite its relative numerical weakness, Louisiana doctrine exercises a considerable influence on the development of the law in Louisiana, in particular, on the private civil law. This doctrine, which is often represented by jurists, especially professors, who are bilingual or trilingual, is a considerable aide to judges, as is evidenced by the numerous citations of doctrine that are scattered throughout the decisions of the courts, especially those of the Supreme Court. Doctrine has also played a great role in the revision of the Civil Code. All the "Books" of the Civil Code have been the object of updates and numerous articles in this code are modified, added, or eliminated each year under the aegis of the Louisiana State Law Institute (LSLI).

Bibliography

Louisiana Pocket Civil Code, 2019 Edition, Carolina Academic Press
See chapters: "Legal History," "Constitutional Framework"

CHAPTER THREE

THE CONSTITUTIONAL FRAMEWORK

In Louisiana, two constitutions establish the constitutional framework for the law: the Constitution of the United States of 1787 (the year it was proposed), and the Constitution of the State of Louisiana of 1974. Each of the fifty states in the union has therefore its own constitution and the union itself has just one. Article VI of the federal constitution establishes the superiority of the federal over a state constitution in case of conflict by stating: "This Constitution, and the Laws of the United States which shall be made in Pursuance thereof; and all Treaties made, or which shall be made, under the Authority of the United States, shall be the supreme Law of the Land; and the Judges in every State shall be bound thereby, any Thing in the Constitution or Laws of any State to the Contrary notwithstanding."

1. CONSTITUTIONS

1.1 PRINCIPAL CHARACTERISTICS OF THE CONSTITUTIONS

The Constitution of (the text in fact reads "for") the United States creates a federal state. It unites all the member states and places the federal government above them, but without entirely supplanting the sovereignty of the member states. Federal supremacy is assured by Article VI, as noted *supra*. The American political system under the federal constitution is neither presidential nor parliamentary; instead it is *sui generis*.

Articles I, II, and III of the federal Constitution provide the principles of the separation of powers and the equality of the three branches of government. The President is elected by universal, indirect suffrage. The citizens of each state choose "a Number of Electors, equal to the whole Number of Senators and Representatives to which the State may be entitled in the Congress." (Constitution, Article II, § 1.) These electors form the electoral college, which then elects the President and the Vice-President. Neither the President nor any member of his administration is responsible before Congress, whose only direct constitutional recourse is through impeachment. The legislative power belongs to Congress, composed of a House of Representatives and a Senate. The voters in the several states elect representatives to a term of two years and senators, two per state, to a term of six years.

The Constitution guarantees fundamental rights. The text announces them in Article I, §§ 9 and 10, in the first ten amendments to the 1787 text (known as the Bill of Rights), the Reconstruction Amendments ratified after the war over secession or Civil War (Amendments 13, 14, and 15), and in other amendments. In addition to these written rights, the Constitution is understood to protect certain unwritten or unenumerated rights that some base in the 9th and 10th Amendments and that others base in a flexible interpretation of due process of law and equal protection of the laws.

The text of the Constitution is rather difficult to amend. Congress may propose an amendment that must then be ratified by three-quarters of the states. And two-thirds of the state legislatures may call a convention that may propose an amendment, which must be ratified by three-quarters of the member states. To date, there have been twenty-seven amendments in all.

The Louisiana Constitution of 1974 provides detailed rules for the powers of the executive (the governor), the powers of the two chambers of the legislature, and the powers of the judiciary. The state Constitution likewise regulates the powers of the sixty-four parishes and of the numerous cities and towns.

1.2 STRUCTURES OF THE FEDERAL STATE AND OF THE STATE OF LOUISIANA

The American Constitution creates a federal state whose political system is plural, not unified. The government instituted by the Constitution possesses a series of "enumerated" legislative powers granted to Congress (Article I, §18), together with very flexible powers to "make all Laws which shall be necessary and proper for carrying into Execution the foregoing Powers, and all other Powers vested by this Constitution in the Government of the United States, or in any Department or Officer thereof." By so providing, the Constitution limits or excludes the ability of member States to act, for example, concerning commerce among the several states which is the exclusive domain of the federal government. The Amendments ratified after the end of the Civil War (1860–1865) increased federal at the expense of state power, most notably in the area of racial discrimination by a member state.

The Louisiana Constitution announces clearly the principle of the separation of the three classic government powers. This principle appears in the first Louisiana Constitution of 1812. But the principle is not as strictly stated as in the federal Constitution.

2. POWERS GRANTED

The federal Constitution creates a federal government of three branches. The Louisiana constitution does likewise.

2.1 LEGISLATIVE POWER

Federal legislative power is bicameral. It is thus allocated to a House of Representatives and to a Senate. The two chambers together compose the Congress. Representatives are elected by universal suffrage in districts whose number is proportional to the population of the district. The term is two years. They number 435. Each State elects two senators, again by universal suffrage, but for a term of six years (17th Amendment (1913)). Before 1913, the State legislatures chose the State's senators. Hence, the two chambers are unequal in their composition and in their constitutional and political roles.

The President also shares the legislative power. After the House and the Senate approve proposed legislation, known as a bill, the bill goes to the President for his signature. If he approves the bill, it becomes law (a statute). If the President disapproves or vetoes the bill, it will only become law if the House and Senate each override the President's veto by a majority of two-thirds. In principle, legislative power is limited to those delegated to Congress by the Constitution. In practice, Congress enjoys great legislative flexibility because of the recognition of incidental and implied powers to legislate in aid of its delegated powers.

In the Louisiana constitution, the legislative power is allocated to two houses, a Senate and a House of Representatives. The members of each house are elected by direct universal suffrage, thirty-nine senators and a maximum of one hundred five representatives. In general, the two houses coordinate their bills, although the House of Representatives has more weight in setting the legislative agenda. For example, the House of Representatives initiates any spending or appropriations bill. If both houses approve a bill by simple majority, the Governor may sign it and the bill becomes law. If the Governor vetoes the bill, the two houses may override the veto by a majority of two-thirds in each house. The Governor, however, possesses a special legislative power: the line-item veto, under which he may veto one or several chapters of an appropriations bill, leaving the rest of the bill intact. In contrast, the President of the United States does not enjoy that power, and the Supreme Court has rejected the attempt by Congress to provide the President with that power.

2.2 EXECUTIVE POWER

The Constitution of the United States places all executive power in the hands of the President. The President is simultaneously head of state and head of the government. He is surrounded by the members of his cabinet, whose number varies. Among the most important members are the Secretary of State (responsible for foreign affairs), the Secretary of Defense, and the Attorney General. The President nominates the members of his cabinet, whose appointments the Senate approves or disapproves.

The President is elected by indirect, universal suffrage. Voters in each State choose presidential electors who will sit in the electoral college (538 members), which establishes a list of the votes cast for president. The list is transmitted to the President of the Senate, who makes it public. A simple majority of the electors in the electoral college chooses the president (270 being the majority). This majority might or might not be a majority of the popular vote. This was the case in November 2016 (and 1824, 1876, 1888, perhaps 1960, and 2000). In fact, the population usually knows the result the evening of the November election. The Vice-President, as running mate of the President, is elected in the same fashion.

The 1787 Constitution did not provide for the creation of Agencies to aid the federal government. These Agencies were created in the years following World War I. They were only subjected to systematic regulation after World War II when Congress enacted the Administrative Procedure Act. Many such federal Agencies enjoy significant independence because their senior officers may only be removed by the President for cause. They play a most important role in several areas, including the economy, interstate commerce, and the environment.

In Louisiana, executive power is mainly in the hands of the Governor, who is elected by universal suffrage for a term of four years. The Governor may be re-elected for a second term. The state constitution limits the number of executive departments to twenty but the legislature may reorganize these departments as it sees fit. Some departments, such as the departments of education and of taxation, are outside the Governor's control. There are also administrative authorities, some under the direction of the Governor, others that are more independent as their members are themselves elected democratically. This is the case for the powerful and influential Public Service Commission, which regulates the plants that produce electricity and gas, especially prices for these services.

2.3 JUDICIAL POWER

Article III of the federal Constitution delegates the judicial power to a single supreme court, but it does not fix the number of judges who will sit on that court. Today, nine Justices are on the court, nominated by the President and confirmed by the Senate, the Chief Justice plus eight Associate Justices. The members of the court enjoy life tenure, and may only be removed through the process of impeachment by the House of Representatives and conviction after trial in and by the Senate.

Article III also empowers Congress to create federal courts inferior to the Supreme Court. There are at present thirteen federal courts of appeal and ninety-four district courts. A court of appeal generally sits in panels of three judges, but the entire court may sit *en banc* as directed by the chief judge of the court. The courts of appeal mostly hear challenges to the decisions of the district courts.

In the district courts, a single judge presides. The district courts hear seven times more civil than criminal cases because there are fewer crimes in federal than under the law of each state. Federal district court judges are assisted by magistrate judges who handle largely procedural questions.

Congress has also created specialized tribunals, such as the U.S. Tax Court, the U.S. Court of Military Appeals, and the U.S. Court of International Trade.

The jurisdiction of the federal courts is defined by Article III § 2 of the Constitution: "The judicial Power shall extend to all Cases, in Law and Equity, arising under this Constitution, the Laws of the United States, and Treaties made, or which shall be made, under their Authority. . . , to Controversies to which the United States shall be a Party . . . , to Controversies between two or more States . . . , between a State and Citizens of another State . . . ." The district courts heard more than 350,000 cases in 2015; the Supreme Court issues about one hundred decisions a year. The most important decision the Supreme Court has ever made is surely *Marbury v. Madison* (1803), in which the Court assumed the power of judicial review, that is, to rule that laws Congress enacts must conform to the Constitution as the Court sees the question and that if they do not they are void.

In Louisiana, there are also three levels within the judicial system: district courts presided by a single judge, courts of appeal (five) on which panels of three judges sit, and a single supreme court of seven justices. All Louisiana judges are elected by universal suffrage within their respective districts. There are also at the trial level courts that are specialized by subject matter, such as family courts, children's courts, criminal courts for minor infractions . . .

Louisiana courts, including the supreme court and the courts of appeal, enjoy plenary jurisdiction, which is presumptively concurrent over matters that might appear at first glance federal in nature, though Congress can provide that federal jurisdiction in certain cases is exclusive. The jurisdiction of Louisiana courts is truly general, for it includes criminal law, civil law, commercial law, and even administrative law. Thus, Louisiana law, as in other American states, does not distinguish between different domains of law and does not divide its courts into different branches as do many legal systems in western Europe.

Bibliography

LEVASSEUR, A., DROIT DES ÉTATS-UNIS (Précis Dalloz, 2d ed., 1994).

LEVASSEUR, A., LE DROIT AMÉRICAIN (Dalloz, Connaissance du Droit 2018).

ZOLLER, E. LES GRANDS ARRÊTS DE LA COUR SUPRÊME DES ÉTATS-UNIS (Dalloz 2010).

CHAPTER FOUR

LEGAL ACTORS

As Montesquieu wrote, "When one visits the Americans and studies their laws, one sees that the authority which they have given to jurists and the influence that jurists have allowed themselves to exert in government form today the most powerful barrier against deviations from democracy. . . . In the United States, jurists form a power that is feared little, that is hardly noticed, that waives no banner for itself . . . that allows itself to go without resistance to all the movements of the social body . . . ."

1. JUDGES

There are, at one and the same time, some important common traits and differences between the status of a federal judge and that of a judge of a federated state.

A first common trait of all American judges is that they belong to a bar association. Nevertheless, that does not mean that only lawyers or legal practitioners can become judges. During the colonial period, and up until the 19th century, judges did not necessarily receive a legal education and were not admitted to a bar association. Today, with some minor exceptions in certain states, all American judges are members of a bar association before becoming judges. Thus, they have all received the same university and professional education. Nevertheless, there is no national or state school for the education of judges such as the national school for the magistracy in France. Because they have been members of a bar association, American judges, then, have practiced as lawyers, as prosecutors, as public defenders or even, though more rarely, as law professors. Ms. Elena Kagan, nominated by President Obama to the Supreme Court, was a law professor, dean of the Harvard Law School, and solicitor general in the Federal Department of Justice.

A second common trait of American judges is that they do not have a "career," properly so called, in the administration of justice. In other words, being a judge in the United States is not a profession, but an occupation, an activity that can just as well be of short duration as it can be for several years, indeed, decades. In this system, if a judge has the ambition to be promoted to a higher level, it would be necessary that this promotion come not through the turning of the internal cogs of the judicial structure but rather from a third person, which could be the electorate or a political authority. The punishment for good or bad conduct by a judge will come from the electorate or from a political authority that would not retain its office indefinitely.

A third common trait of American judges is that they are the personalization of a political reality. They have been either elected to offices for which they have been candidates or nominated by a political authority which is itself an emanation of the electorate. Thus, it is the people who, directly or indirectly, chose its judges.

There are two categories of federal judges: on the one side, the judges called "Article III (of the Constitution) judges" and, on the other side, the judges appointed within the framework of Article I of the Constitution. Besides these, there are federal magistrates.

Article III (of the Constitution) federal judges are appointed by the President of the United States with the advice and consent of the Senate. These judges are appointed for life and can be dismissed from their offices only by the procedure of impeachment. It is essential that the candidate possess the legal qualifications required to occupy the prestigious position of federal judge. The President is often influenced in his choice by his political allies. Judges of federal courts other than the Article III courts are appointed by the President with the consent of the Senate. These judges are, in general, appointed for a period of 15 years. As a general rule, their nomination is not covered by the media, for the process of their nomination does not provoke great controversies. Federal magistrates are appointed by the judges of the federal district courts for a renewable term of eight years. The judges choose these magistrates from among the lawyers who have a long experience and a good reputation and who are recommended by a selection committee. The magistrates are charged with presiding over the preliminary hearings of a suit, whether it be civil or criminal. They can likewise sit as a judge in minor criminal matters and, with the consent of the parties, in civil affairs.

In Louisiana, all the judges are elected. A candidate for one of the five courts of appeal or for the supreme court must have practiced law for ten or eight years, depending on the court. The supreme court, composed of seven judges, has jurisdiction over all matters, civil (as to both fact and law) and criminal, but, regarding the latter, solely for questions of legal interpretation. The appellate courts are composed of three judges. They have jurisdiction, on appeal, in civil and family matters and have a power of control over jury verdicts in criminal matters. The district courts sit as single judges. They have jurisdiction in both civil and criminal matters. The Louisiana court judges are assisted by one or two law clerks. This very prized position is sought by recent graduates of the law schools. Moreover, in each district a district attorney—a procurator or public minister—is elected for six years. He initiates criminal actions within his district and is the legal counsel to the grand jury.

2. CLERKS OF COURT

The clerk of court is an official of the court. He performs numerous administrative responsibilities in addition to his judicial obligations, for which he answers to the court. He keeps all the files up to date, inscribes the suits in the records of the court, assures the proper running of hearings, facilitates communications with lawyers, and administers the oaths of jurors and witnesses. The clerk of court is also the public representative of the court.

In order to be a clerk of court, it is necessary to have a high school degree and a certificate from a professional school, preferably on legal subjects. Some courts require a degree in business administration. A clerk of court can enjoy a lengthy career by being promoted within the hierarchy of the courts of the state.

3. LAWYERS, ATTORNEYS AT LAW

Before becoming an attorney at law or lawyer, it is necessary to fulfill the conditions of professional formation, which are obtaining a basic degree, in general the JD (*Juris Doctor*), which is awarded by a law school that has been accredited by the ABA (American Bar Association), and passing the Louisiana bar examination. The Louisiana Supreme Court exercises a power of oversight over the organization of the examination by the bar association. Once enrolled in the state bar association, the lawyer or attorney at law must pay the expenses of his enrollment in the bar in order to obtain his license. Later, he will take an oath before the supreme court. Holding a basic degree, such as the JD, and enrollment in a local bar association implies that only lawyers are authorized to be legal practitioners. In the conduct of his profession, the lawyer is subjected to very strict ethical rules. The Model Code of Professional Responsibility adopted by the ABA has served as the model for the Rules that have been adopted by the bar associations of the states, including Louisiana.

Remuneration, or lawyer fees, can be fixed according to the duration of the work (billable hour) or conditional—contingency fees—which means that a client will not pay his attorney unless the latter wins the case.

The Supreme Court of the United States, relying on the 1st Amendment to the Constitution, has concluded that the majority of the regulations that the states had established forbidding lawyers from advertising their services are unconstitutional. There has resulted from this a fierce competition between law firms, which has permitted persons of modest means to benefit from the war over legal fees.

Lawyers can conduct their professions in various forms. Many lawyers are in private practice and conduct their professions either alone or in a group or firm. Some lawyers hold the title of in-house counsel, because they belong to the legal department of a juridical person. Likewise, many lawyers are in the service of governments. Alongside these traditional forms of legal practice, a new form of furnishing legal services has been established: legal clinics. They deal with ordinary matters, those with which clients of modest means are often confronted, such as matters of divorce, alimentary support, leases . . . .

At the level of the federal government, a great number of US Attorneys and lawyers conduct their professions in the agencies of the federal government. At the head of the federal Department of Justice, the Attorney General is a member of the President's cabinet. The Attorney General is named by the President and is subjected to the advice and consent of the Senate. He is assisted by US Attorneys, who exercise their responsibilities in the 94 districts that have been established in the 50 states and the District of Columbia. The duty of a US District Attorney is to assure respect for federal law in civil and criminal matters.

There are numerous posts for jurists in the federal agencies, such as the Federal Trade Commission, the National Labor Relations Board, the CIA, the IRS . . . .

In Louisiana, a state Attorney General is at the head of the Department of Justice. Like the Governor, he is elected by the voters of the state. The state Attorney General represents the State of Louisiana in civil and criminal matters that fall within the jurisdiction of the state.

At the local level, the counties or parishes and urban areas or cities are represented by prosecutors called county attorneys, county prosecutors, or still district attorneys (DA) and urban areas or cities by city attorneys.

4. NOTARIES

The notary in the states of the United States, including Louisiana, is the not the equivalent of a French notary. A notary in Louisiana can be any person who is 18 years old, without a criminal record, and a resident of the State of Louisiana, which is where he conducts his activities. This person must have taken several law courses and notarial practice courses, courses often taken by correspondence; he must have passed an examination in order to receive his commission in the form of the seal of the state government. It is not rare to see notaries in large shopping centers where their services can be solicited in order, for example, to authenticate signatures. The principal activities of notaries are to certify or authenticate signatures on acts of donation, acknowledgements of debts . . . . They also take oaths regarding the identity of authors and witnesses of legal documents.

5. BAILIFFS

A bailiff is a public officer whose essential charge is to assure order and security in the courts. The bailiff assists the judge and the jury as well as the public. He precedes the judge into the hearing room and declares in a loud voice that the judge is entering the hearing room, so that members of the public may stand to their feet out of respect for the justice that the judge represents. The bailiff assures the good conduct and security of hearings, and he accompanies the jury in order to prevent any contact between them and third persons and to assure the safe-keeping and protection of the jury. He can be called upon to serve executory acts and acts of procedure on certain persons, such as debtors of alimentary support. To become a bailiff, it is necessary to be at least 18 years old, to be a citizen of the United States, and, at a minimum, to have a high school degree or its equivalent. It is recommended that he have taken some courses in the administration of justice at a professional school and to have interned in a correctional facility.

6. BUSINESS LAWYERS

Many business entities have created, within these businesses themselves, their own legal departments, which are composed of in-house counsels or business lawyers. These jurists are lawyers who must be enrolled in the register of the bar association of their place of work and, by virtue of this, are subjected to the same code of ethics as are the lawyers who work in law firms. The chief of the legal department as a general rule bears the name of 'general counsel.' More and more, essentially for financial reasons, business entities prefer to be represented before the courts by their in-house counsels rather than by external lawyers and law firms.

CHAPTER FIVE

CRIMINAL LAW

1. SUBSTANTIVE CRIMINAL LAW

The scope of federal criminal law is limited by its purpose which is to vest in the federal government the responsibility and the duty to assure the prosecution of crimes that undermine the sovereignty of the United States. Its principal concern bears on violations of the law concerning national boundaries as well as the boundaries between the member states, as is the case today with national policy regarding immigrants. It also concerns violations that a single state cannot easily confront because the problem is national and transcends state borders such as, for example, traffic in illegal drugs. It follows that the member states of the Union have the primary jurisdiction over criminal law.

After the United States purchased Louisiana from France in 1803, to limit the influence of the unwritten Anglo-American common law, Louisiana declared that all crimes shall be defined, from now on, by its state legislature. This was the purpose of legislation enacted in 1805. The fifty-two articles of this law, written in both French and English, defined crimes, announced penalties, and set out criminal procedure. Edward Livingston produced a famous draft penal code in 1824 that the legislature rejected. It was only in 1942 that a true Criminal Code was adopted. This Code, as amended, remains in force today. It represents a very important transition, even a departure, from a largely unwritten criminal law derived from the common law and a law only partially written and set down in separate texts. The 1942 Code, in contrast, marked the arrival in Louisiana of a regime of not only written but codified criminal law.

Title 14, Chapter 1 of the Revised Statutes makes up the Criminal Code. The Code of substantive criminal law consists of eight parts; the Code of Criminal Procedure, enacted in 1966, is a separate text. The preliminary provisions of the Criminal Code contain a long series of definitions, quite typical of legislation in the common-law tradition, as well as instructions on methods of interpreting the Criminal Code.

Among the twelve definitions given, we will mention the general distinction between felonies and misdemeanors, which is based on the duration of imprisonment, with forced labor, much as in common law. The definition of "another person" includes those juridical persons that have the legal capacity to commit crimes and are subject to fine.

Definition #11 states that an unborn child is a human being as of fertilization and implantation until birth. The Code distinguishes between crimes that require "specific intent" to cause the consequences of the prohibited conduct and those that require only a "general intent" to commit a crime, meaning that the actor ought to have anticipated the particular consequences of the conduct when those consequences in fact did occur.

A good ten articles deal with the various sorts of culpability. Any person under the age of ten years enjoys absolute immunity from prosecution. Any person under the age of seventeen may not be prosecuted criminally, except for crimes that are subject to capital punishment or that involve sexual aggression. Likewise, a person incapable of criminal intent because of mental illness cannot be prosecuted, meaning that the person cannot distinguish right from wrong, which leaves the presiding judge considerable flexibility. Voluntary intoxication and voluntary use of drugs do not eliminate culpability, unless the defendant was incapable of being motivated by the specific intent required as an element of the crime or lacked the specific knowledge required in the definition of a certain crime.

The Code recognizes other means of defense, such as duress, physical impossibility, and the legal exercise of a public function or of a domestic authority. Using defensive force is permitted so long as doing so is reasonable and apparently justified under the circumstances to defend one's person or property. This is above all the case when defensive force results in a homicide. Here again the judge may evaluate the circumstances and the reasonableness of the use of force based on subjective factors, such as age, sex, and mental condition of the aggressor and of the victim. The Code adds as defenses both error of fact and error of law. If the law permits, error of fact occurs when there is error as to a fact or ignorance of a fact when the law defines the offense to include accurate knowledge of that fact as a "mental element" of the crime. Ignorance of the law, however, is not a defense. At the limit, it may be pleaded in two situations: first, if the defendant could have justifiably believed that the legislature had repealed the relevant statute and, second, if the defendant could have reasonably believed that a judgment of the highest court had declared unconstitutional the relevant provision of the law to be applied in his case.

Generally, every crime includes two essential elements: a moral element described by the Latin term *mens rea*; and a material element described by the term *actus reus.*

There are five principal crimes against the person (R.S. 14:29, Part 2). Homicide is divided in two categories: murder or intentional homicide and unintentional homicide. Murder or intentional homicide with premeditation is first degree murder when the defendant had the specific intent to kill or to wound very seriously his victim while at the same time committing another extremely serious crime, such as armed robbery or an act of terrorism. In the past, murders in the first degree could receive capital punishment. The federal Supreme Court's decisions have moved most first degree murders to the category of second degree murder. Involuntary homicide is one step down in seriousness, because here the element of premeditation is absent. This murder in the second degree is also called voluntary manslaughter and includes murders with the intent to kill or to wound seriously. Nevertheless, they are in general committed in a "sudden passion or heat of blood." Assault and battery is treated in section 33 of Title 14. Battery is defined as the intentional use of force or violence against another person or the intentional administration of a poison or other toxic substance to another person. Aggravated battery occurs if the defendant commits battery using a dangerous weapon. Assault is the attempt to strike another person to cause injury or to produce in another person the reasonable fear that such blows may occur. These definitions are followed by a list of persons whose status or profession may increase or diminish the penalties for such acts (members of a police force, teachers, family members . . .). Under the law of 1805, rape was a capital crime, as in the common law. The Criminal Code of 1942 distinguished three grades of rape. First degree rape occurs against a person of at least sixty-five years of age who was not able to offer the least resistance. Second degree rape occurs against a victim under sixty-five years of age, also unable to offer resistance or incapable of understanding the situation because the defendant had drugged the victim beforehand. The sentence may be from five to forty years in prison at hard labor. Third degree rape occurs if the victim is intoxicated and the perpetrator knew or should have known this fact. Here the sentence may not exceed twenty-five years. Other crimes against the person include kidnaping or false imprisonment (R.S. 14:44) and defamation (R.S. 14:47).

A second list deals with crimes against property, for example, criminal arson and use of explosives (RS 14:51), aggravated criminal damage to property of another (a pipeline, growing crops, etc.) (RS 14:55), simple and aggravated burglary (RS 14:60 & 62) (without or with a dangerous weapon), and criminal trespass (RS 14:63).

Finally, we will mention several crimes against the public, such as: the illegal carrying of a weapon (RS 14:94), the aggravated obstruction of a highway of commerce (road, navigable waterway, railroad . . .), operating a motor vehicle while intoxicated or under the influence of drugs (including a boat, airplane...), hit-and-run (RS 14:99.1 & 100), cruelty to animals, illegal contact sports ("tough-man" contests) (RS 14:102.11), disturbing the peace (e.g., by a "fistic" encounter) (RS 14:103)... The Criminal Code also targets several types of crimes against the State or against the government. Articles RS 14:113 et seq. define treason and other acts of disloyalty to the United States and to the State of Louisiana. Perjury is punished by Articles RS 14:123 et seq. The Code proscribes bribery and intimidation of public officers, witnesses, and members of juries under Articles RS 14:118 et seq.

2. CRIMINAL PROCEDURE

The doctrine of home rule in North-American common law requires that the administration of criminal justice occur at the local level, as near the place of the crime as possible, by persons elected locally or chosen by local political institutions. This doctrine is linked to the role of jury, which likewise calls upon "locals" to judge crimes committed locally. In addition, this doctrine is guided by a concern to preserve local autonomy against the central administration both at the state and federal levels. Here one can see the distrust Americans have for executive power and the oppression that a central power can wield.

Police officers are in general recruited within each parish (or county in the states of the common law) or each municipality. The person who conducts criminal prosecutions is a lawyer elected as district attorney for a renewable term. His authority is nearly exclusive to decide to prosecute a particular defendant and for what crime and in what degree. Indeed, the district attorney may negotiate with the accused willing to plead guilty to a lesser offense. Such "plea bargaining" has been recognized by the Supreme Court of the United States as an essential component of the American criminal justice system.

The investigation is conducted together by the local district attorney, the local police (which is independent of the district attorney), and investigators, with the goal of bringing to light the facts surrounding the crime, which may then be presented first to a grand jury and then to a petit or trial jury. Thus, the decision to prosecute a particular defendant for a felony belongs to the grand jury, not to the district attorney. (Code Crim. Proc., Title 12.) A petit or trial jury must be empaneled in any crime for which capital punishment is possible (twelve jurors deciding unanimously), a crime for which the punishment must be imprisonment at hard labor (twelve jurors by majority of ten), and a crime for which punishment could be imprisonment at hard labor (six jurors unanimously).

The trial in American law is much more important than the corresponding procedure in France, for example. The trial is truly the crucial moment in the course of the proceeding, during which the whole truth is to be revealed by direct and exclusive reliance on the proof presented. Neither the grand jury, nor the district attorney, nor the police are obligated to present all the circumstances that surround the alleged crime. This is true of all the facts that might tend to incriminate or might tend to exonerate the defendant. Under the adversary character of the American justice system, the prosecuting attorney presents the elements of his case against the defendant, who then presents his own version of the facts and his defense. The entire procedure is structured around fundamental guarantees to the defendant against errors that might undermine the correct determination of his guilt. Among those guarantees are the right to the assistance of legal counsel, the right to a jury (Louisiana Constitution Art. 1 §17), the right to confront and to cross-examine witnesses testifying against him, the right to call his own witnesses, and above all the right not to be compelled to testify against himself (Federal Constitution, Fifth Amendment). As stated in Article I-2 of the Declaration of Rights in the Louisiana Constitution, no one may be deprived of his life, liberty, or property without due process of law. The presumption of innocence and the requirement that the prosecution must prove its case beyond a reasonable doubt are the pillars of criminal procedure. Moreover, many rules quite technical in nature protect the jury from the presentation of proof that would be prejudicial to the defendant (e.g., the hearsay rule) and might influence the jury to the detriment of the presumption of innocence. The jury's role today remains the determination of the facts after presentation of proofs and arguments by counsel. It is interesting to note that the prosecution makes its argument to the jury last after having presented its case first. The burden of proof weighs so heavily on the prosecution that it is legitimate for the prosecutor to be last to speak before the jury retires to deliberate. After the final arguments, the judge charges the jury on the law that it is to apply in the case. Then the jury deliberates alone, without any other person present. Its verdict is either guilty or not guilty. In almost all cases, it is the judge who pronounces the sentence.

The role of the victim in criminal procedure is surprisingly minor, even non-existent. The victim may not commence criminal proceedings, nor may he intervene in a case already begun by the prosecutor. In other words, there is no *partie civile* in American procedure as there is in French criminal procedure. Nevertheless, the victim may begin his own civil case for damages against the defendant before, during, or after the criminal case.

Bibliography

Revised Statutes 14: 1 et seq.
Louisiana Code of Criminal Procedure

CHAPTER SIX

PERSONS

The term "person" is not defined in the Louisiana Civil Code. However, relying on the opinions of commentators, an accepted definition of the term in the law of Louisiana is "that which is capable of having rights and obligations."

1. DISTINCTION BETWEEN NATURAL PERSONS AND JURIDICAL PERSONS

According to Louisiana Civil Code (La. Civ.) article 24: "There are two kinds of persons: natural persons and juridical persons." A natural person is a human being. A juridical person is an entity to which the law attributes personality, such as a corporation or a partnership. The inherent differences in these two types of persons justify the existence of different rules for each type, particularly as regards the beginning and the end of their respective legal personalities.

As a general rule, "[n]atural personality commences at the moment of live birth." La. Civ. Code art. 25. Live birth is defined in the Louisiana Vital Statistics Laws as follows:

[A] birth in which the child shows evidence of life after complete birth. A birth is complete when the child is entirely outside the mother, even if the umbilical cord is uncut and the placenta still attached. The words "evidence of life" include heart action, breathing, or movement of voluntary muscles.

Note, however, that the child need not be born capable of living. Although the general rule provides for natural personality beginning at live birth, "[a]n unborn child is considered as a natural person for whatever relates to its interests from the moment of conception." La. Civ. Code art. 26. Such is the rule provided the child is later born alive: "If the child is born dead, it shall be considered never to have existed except for purposes of actions resulting from its wrongful death." *Id.* In other words, aside from the wrongful death context, the child's natural personality is retroactively erased if he or she is not born alive.

Questions arise regarding the definition of the term "conception" particularly in the case of assisted reproductive technology. Special legislation provides that a human embryo (defined as an in vitro fertilized human ovum composed of one or more living human cells and human genetic material so unified and organized that it will develop in utero into an unborn child, La. R.S. 9:121) exists as a juridical person until implanted or at any other time when rights attach to an unborn child in accordance with law. La. R.S. 9:123. Other special legislation grants rights to a child who is conceived after the death of a decedent who specifically authorized in writing his surviving spouse to use his gametes, provided the child is born to the surviving spouse using the gametes of the decedent within three years of his death. La. R.S. 9:391.1.

"Natural personality terminates at death." La. Civ. Code art. 25. Death can be physical—(1) where a physician determines that a person experiences an irreversible cessation of spontaneous respiratory and circulatory functions, (2) in the event that artificial means of support preclude such a determination, where a physician determines that a person experiences an irreversible total cessation of brain function, or (3) a person is pronounced dead by a coroner based on personal observations, information, or statements obtained from specified personnel at the scene reporting from firsthand observation. La. R.S. 9:111. Beyond physical death, "[w]hen a person has disappeared under circumstances such that his death seems certain, his death is considered to have been established even though his body has not been found." La. Civ. Code art. 30. Additionally, an absent person (defined by Louisiana Civil Code Article 47 as "one who has no representative in this state and whose whereabouts are not known and cannot be ascertained by diligent effort") who has been so for five years is presumed to be dead. La. Civ. Code art. 54. Finally, one who is on active duty in one of the armed services of the United States who has been reported missing under circumstances which have induced the armed service to which he was attached to accept the presumption of his death shall be presumed dead under the laws of the state. La. R.S. 9:1441.

Natural persons are so identified in Louisiana law on the basis of a variety of criteria. Some are inherent to the person, i.e., citizenship, gender, name, domicile, age, and health. Citizenship links a person to his or her country. Gender links a person to the status of male or female. Name individualizes a person. Domicile (defined as a residence with intent to remain) provides a location for the person with respect to legal issues such as recordation, venue, subject matter jurisdiction, and others. Age is relevant for classifying a person as being of "age," a major, as opposed to being a minor; age is also relevant for determining the ability to discern. Health issues could lead to interdiction, continuing tutorship, or to classifying a person as deprived of reason. Other identification elements are linked to a natural person's familial status, i.e., married, filiated. Marital status is important in various areas of law, particularly tax, community property, and inheritance. Filiation is the legal relationship between a child and his or her parent and may occur by proof of maternity or paternity or by adoption. La. Civ. Code art. 178. This implicates a host of legal issues, particularly inheritance, tutorship, child support, and other alimentary obligations.

The rules governing the legal personality of a juridical person are different from those that are applicable to natural persons. Some juridical persons are "public" while others are "private." The legal personality of most juridical persons begins when the entity is created. Depending on the type of juridical person at issue, creation may result from the will of the persons creating it or from registration with the Louisiana Secretary of State (an elected official housed within the executive branch of the state government). Legal personality of most juridical persons ends upon their dissolution or possibly with their liquidation.

Juridical persons share some identification criteria with natural persons: they have a name and a domicile. These, however, are dependent on the private will of those concerned, as opposed to public order.

2. RIGHTS ATTACHED TO PERSONALITY UNDER THE LOUISIANA CIVIL CODE

The primary legal effect of personality is capacity. There are two types of capacity in Louisiana law: capacity of enjoyment (also called general legal capacity) and capacity of exercise (also called capacity to enter into juridical acts). All natural persons have the capacity of enjoyment which is the capacity to be vested with rights and duties. La. Civ. Code art. 27. However, as a general rule, "[a] natural person who has reached majority (18 years of age in Louisiana, La. Civ. Code art. 29) has capacity to make all sorts of juridical acts. . . ." La. Civ. Code art. 28.

One must point out that legislation provides many exceptions to the general rule regarding the capacity of exercise. For example, minors who have been emancipated have the capacity of exercise. (*See, e.g.*, La. Civ. Code art. 1918 depriving capacity to contract to *unemancipated* minors.) Also, certain minors have the capacity to enter certain contracts of donation in favor of certain people. La. Civ. Code art. 1476. On the other side of the spectrum, some majors—interdicts and persons deprived of reason—lack the capacity of exercise. A full interdict (a major or emancipated minor judicially ordered as such because of an infirmity that renders him or her unable consistently to make reasoned decisions regarding the care of his or her person and property, or to communicate those decisions and whose interests cannot be protected by less restrictive means, La. Civ. Code art. 389) has a court-appointed curator who represents him in juridical acts and cares for his person or affairs. La. Civ. Code art. 392. A limited interdict (a major or emancipated minor judicially ordered as such because of an infirmity that renders him unable consistently to make reasoned decisions regarding the care of his or her person or property or any aspect of either, or to communicate those decisions, La. Civ. Code art. 390) is represented by a curator in certain aspects as detailed by the order of limited interdiction. La. Civ. Code art. 392. Juridical acts entered in violation of the aforementioned rules are relatively null and, as a general rule, may be rescinded by the interdict's legal representative. La. Civ. Code art. 1919.

Besides these basic rights which can be said to be of a "civil law" nature, one must add the rights which the Constitution of the United States and the Bill of Rights grant to all citizens such as: freedom of religion, freedom of expression, right to one's privacy…In addition, Article 1 of the Declaration of Rights of the Constitution of Louisiana lists twenty six rights which belong to persons and it requires the government to ensure the protection of those rights as well as the well-being of all.

The capacity of exercise is a primary reason for creating a juridical person or entity since the legal personality of the juridical person is distinct from the legal personality of each one of its individual members. Of course, the rights and obligations of the juridical person are achieved through its representatives. Nevertheless, in most cases, the members will not be personally liable for the conduct of the juridical person.

Bibliography

Louisiana Pocket Civil Code, 2018 Edition, Carolina Academic Press

CHAPTER SEVEN

THE FAMILY

1. CONJUGAL UNIONS

In Louisiana law, marriage is the only legal form of conjugality. Marriage is defined by Article 86 of the Civil Code as "a legal relationship between a man and a woman that is created by civil contract." The United States Supreme Court has ruled that state-law must recognize marriages contracted between persons of the same sex. (Obergefell v. Hodges, 2015.) As of this writing, the Louisiana legislature is considering an amendment to Article 86 to conform to the command of that case. This legal relationship has no religious character; a religious contract of marriage is without legal effect, even if it parallels the civil contract. Marriage does not create a juridical person distinct from the spouses themselves. In this way, marriage differs from ordinary partnerships. The special nature of the contract of marriage permits the State, through legislation, to modify the obligations that the contract of marriage creates without violating State or Federal constitutional limitations on modifying contracts in general. (La. Const. Art. I §23; U. S. Const. Art. I §10.)

Three requirements must be met for the contract of marriage to be valid. First, there must be no legal impediment to the marriage, such as the continuing marriage of one of the spouses to another person, or kinship between the spouses within the fourth degree (collaterals, including half-brothers and sisters, and ascendants and descendants). Second, a third person must celebrate the marriage and the celebrant must be qualified by law to do so; for example a judge or a priest or some other religious leader. Third, the spouses must be physically present at the ceremony; marriages by proxy are not permitted. During the ceremony the spouses must express their free consent. The consent is not free if given by a person incapable of understanding what marriage is, for example, because of intoxication or mental disease. Nor is it free if there is a vice of consent such as duress. The Civil Code does not set a minimum age for the validity of marriage. A minor may marry with the consent of his two parents or of his tutor, or with the approval of the juvenile court. If one or both spouses are minors who marry without this consent, the Civil Code provides the rule that marriage emancipates a minor.

Marriage creates **personal effects** in the form of duties owed by each spouse to the other. Article 98 states first the duty of fidelity. Marriage also creates a duty of mutual assistance, especially in case of infirmity or illness. But the Civil Code does not create a duty of cohabitation, and each spouse may have his own domicile. During marriage, a spouse may bring a civil action against the other outside a suit to dissolve the marriage. Marriage does not change the name of either spouse; they may use the family name or surname of either spouse or a combination of those names. (La. Civ. Code Art. 100.)

Marriage also creates **patrimonial effects**. For most marriages these include the legal regime of a community of acquets and gains, which applies unless the spouses choose a different regime before they marry. Under this regime, goods acquired by onerous contract during marriage by either spouse enter the community. All salaries earned by either spouse also become community property, as do the natural and civil fruits even of a thing that is the separate property of one of the spouses. Separate property includes goods that each spouse brings to the marriage as well as gifts and bequests received during marriage. Under the legal regime of community of acquets and gains, the debts of either spouse are presumptively debts of the community and therefore all assets in the community may be seized to satisfy them.

Louisiana law does recognize a form of conjugal union that does have a religious foundation, namely, covenant marriage. Spouses may choose this form of marriage by a declaration before a notary. As compared to an ordinary marriage, a covenant marriage is more difficult to dissolve through a no-fault divorce, but for a divorce based on fault is quite similar.

Spouses enjoy the freedom to organize their matrimonial property regime as they see fit within the constraints of the public order. Thus, they cannot modify the order of succession established by law, nor may they modify the marital portion (La. Civ. Code Art. 2433 et seq.). Within the community property regime, spouses may not by agreement limit the capacity of one spouse to act unilaterally with regard to the community property.

Spouses may choose a separate property regime or a mixed regime of separate and community property. Under a separate property regime, if a spouse incurs an obligation for necessaries for himself or for the family, the other spouse is solidarily liable for the debt. Once married, spouses may modify their matrimonial regime, but only with the approval of the court.

2. DISSOLUTION

Article 101 of the Civil Code provides for only three ways to end a marriage. Divorce is the most often used, and no-fault divorce is the most common type. To obtain a judgment of divorce without fault, the spouses must live separately for a period of time: 180 days if there are no minor children of the marriage, 365 days if there are. Fault as a basis for divorce is adultery by the other spouse, the conviction and sentencing of the other spouse for commission of a felony, and physical or sexual abuse by the other spouse.

A judicial declaration of nullity also ends a marriage. In the case of relative nullity caused by a vice of consent, the civil effects of the marriage continue after the declaration of nullity is pronounced.

Among the civil effects that continue are the legitimacy of any child of the marriage and the obligation of support through alimony. A marriage may also be declared absolutely null if there was no marriage ceremony. But even a marriage absolutely null *ab initio* may be deemed a putative marriage and may produce civil effects for the innocent spouse and, above all, for the children. For there to be a putative marriage, one spouse must have had a good faith belief that the marriage ceremony in fact occurred or that there was no other impediment to the marriage.

3. FILIATION AND PARENTAGE

Filiation is the legal relationship between a child and his parent (La. Civ. Code art. 178). Filiation is established in two ways: biological filiation by proof of maternity or paternity, and adoptive filiation by proof of adoption of the child. As for maternity, it is proved by a preponderance of the evidence. Proof of paternity may occur in several ways. The paternity of the husband of the mother is presumed if the child is born during the marriage. This presumption of paternity also obtains if the child is born within 300 days after the end of the marriage. This presumption derives from the well-known presumption in Roman law "*pater is est quem nuptiae demonstrant*" but is less absolute. If the mother of the child remarries before the child is born, this second marriage may produce two presumptions of paternity. To avoid this dilemma, the Civil Code presumes that the first husband is the father. Nevertheless, that husband may obtain a judgment of disavowal, in which case the second husband will be presumed to be the father. The second husband may in turn within the year following the judgment of disavowal of the first husband bring his own action in disavowal.

There are three other, somewhat weaker, presumptions of paternity. First, a man may, by authentic act and without the consent of the mother, acknowledge the paternity of a child who is not filiated to another man. This presumption imposes on the father a duty of support of the child. Second, a man is presumed to be the father of a child if scientific tests establish biological paternity by a probability of 99.9%. Finally, a presumption of paternity exists if the mother of the child identifies the man as the father but only with the goal of providing child support.

When filiation is contested by action, proof must be by clear and convincing evidence, more than a preponderance. This action prescribes in one year. When the husband of the mother consents to her artificial insemination, he may not bring an action to disavow paternity.

An essential effect of the establishment of filiation is the obligation of both mother and father to support the child. This obligation in general ends upon the majority of the child but may be extended if the child pursues advanced studies. During the minority of the child, and as long as they are married, the parents possess parental authority. They exercise this authority over the person of the child to assure his protection as well as his education, both practical and moral. The parents administer the patrimony of their minor child. They may delegate this authority only in the cases provided by law.

4. SUCCESSIONS

Upon the death by natural causes of a person, her patrimony, made up of assets (active) and debts (passive), forms a universality, and Louisiana law uses the term of art "estate" to identify this universality. The word "succession" denotes the mode of transmission of this universality. Nevertheless, Louisiana law continues to embrace the principle by which the successors of the deceased are seized of the ownership of the estate immediately upon his death (*le mort saisit le vif*), despite the fact that the administration of the succession is slow and complex.

Louisiana law recognizes two kinds of successor. First, the universal successor represents the deceased and enters into possession of all of his rights and obligations. The universal successor may be an heir or a universal or general legatee. Second, the successor may succeed by particular title, in which case he succeeds only to rights concerning certain assets.

A succession may be either intestate (or legal) or testamentary. A succession is intestate when the deceased leaves no testament. If the deceased leaves a testament but the testament fails to deal with a certain item in the estate, the rules of intestate or legal succession apply.

The Civil Code classifies the relatives of the deceased in four hierarchical categories: (1) descendants; (2) ascendants; (3) surviving spouse; and (4) collaterals. Relatives in a higher category exclude those in a lower category. To determine the degree of relationship that separate the deceased from a successor, one counts the generations that separate the two. Thus, there are three degrees of relationship between an uncle and his nephew. Successors of the same degree share by head. Louisiana recognizes the theory of representation of a deceased by his heirs, his children in particular. Successors who succeed by representation take their share of the estate by root (*per stirpes*). Children or their representatives exclude all other heirs. If there is no child but there is a surviving spouse, that surviving spouse succeeds to the half of the community of acquets and gains that belonged to the deceased. If the deceased left descendants, the surviving spouse succeeds to the decedent's share of the community in usufruct and the descendants succeed to its naked ownership. This usufruct of the surviving spouse continues until death or remarriage. The separate property of a spouse in community, or goods acquired by spouses who are separate in property are transmitted in several ways if there are no children of the marriage. Three illustrations may be presented: (1) if the deceased without descendant is survived by a parent and by a sibling, the parent receives a usufruct and the sibling the naked ownership; (2) if the deceased leaves neither descendant nor parent, the surviving spouse succeeds to the exclusion of any other ascendant or collateral; (3) if the deceased leaves no descendant, no parent, no sibling, and no surviving spouse, the other ascendants succeed. In that last case, the ascendants are divided into maternal and paternal lines and share the estate equally.

A testamentary succession requires that the deceased have made a testament in olographic or notarial form (La. Civ. Code art. 1574). In Louisiana, the freedom of testation is limited. The principal traditional limitation imposed by law is the existence of forced heirship in two cases: first and mainly, the forced portion that goes to children under the age of twenty-three, second the forced portion that benefits children of any age who are incapable, for physical or mental causes, to care for themselves or to manage their patrimony.

An heir may accept a testamentary succession under benefit of inventory (La. Civ. Code art. 1604), which permits him only to be liable for succession debts up to the value of the active portion of the estate that he will receive.

Bibliography

Louisiana Pocket Civil Code, 2018 Edition, Carolina Academic Press

CHAPTER EIGHT

PROPERTY

1. SCOPE OF PROPERTY

One who takes on the task of describing in the French language « le domaine des biens », such as this concept exists in Louisiana law, will face a linguistic challenge. The source of the difficulty is that in Louisiana, whose language of the law is English, there is no equivalent, in the Louisiana Civil Code, for this French expression, "le droit des biens." The concept "le droit des biens" corresponds more exactly in the English language to the expression « the law of *property* ». If one wishes to describe « le domaine des biens » in Louisiana law, one must concentrate on the sense of this key word: property.

In Louisiana law, the term "property" is used in two different, but also overlapping, senses. The first sense is that of certain "things"; the second is that of certain "rights," some but not all.

Used in the sense of certain "things," the word "property" signifies "susceptible of appropriation," that is, things on which a person can have a right. Certain things cannot become the object of either ownership or of any other right. They are things that the Louisiana Civil Code calls "common" things, such as the air and the high seas, things that cannot be appropriated. .

In the Louisiana Civil Code there are numerous classifications of these certain "things." Among the most important one can cite "public things," (owned by the government in its public capacity) which are distinguished from "private" things (property of private individuals or of the state acting in the capacity of a private individual). "Immovables" (land and its component parts, such as buildings and other constructions) are differentiated from "movables." Things that can be consumed or are exhausted in the course of being used are opposed to things which cannot be consumed; "fruits," things that renew themselves, are opposed to "products," which diminish the substance of their source.

The Louisiana Civil Code also makes a distinction between "corporeal" things and "incorporeal" things, the latter being deprived of material substance (having no corpus or body), as is the case with a variety of rights, such as servitudes. It can also be a matter of "rights" or "titles" that bear on corporeal things. It is necessary likewise to mention incorporeal things or rights that are grouped under the concept of "intellectual property" (propriété intellectuelle), such as patents, copyrights and trademarks. These incorporeal things are of particular juridical importance in matters of successions and in the distribution of assets in matrimonial regimes.

The word "property" can be used in the sense of certain rights. In the large sense, the word "property" includes all patrimonial rights, that is, rights that are susceptible of having a pecuniary value. Thereby excluded are all personal rights which do not have a commercial or monetary value, such as the right to vote and certain family rights such as the duty of fidelity. In its restrained sense, the word "property" bears on one subset of patrimonial rights—the category of "real rights," which are rights that confer particular powers over a thing (including a right of "pursuit") and that are "opposable to the world," to the exclusion of credit or personal rights.

2. POWERS OVER THINGS

Louisiana law recognizes two types of powers over things: powers that exist in *right* and powers that exist in *fact*.

In the words of La. Civ. Code art. 476: "One may have various rights in things: 1. Ownership; 2. Personal and predial servitudes; and 3. Such other real rights as the law allows." In short, then, the powers as of right are the various real rights.

The Louisiana right of ownership is like the Roman right of ownership, in that it is divided into three sub-real rights: *usus*, *fructus*, and *abusus*. *Usus* is the right to make use of the thing, to draw from it its economics advantages. *Fructus* is the right to receive and to take the fruits (if any) that the thing gives, be they natural or civil fruits. *Abusus* is the right to dispose of the thing, in particular, to alienate it.

The right of ownership is subject to various sorts of modifications. Two of them deserve special mention: ownership "in indivision" (or "co-ownership") and ownership "in trust."

There is indivision when the thing is "the property of two or more persons"(La. Civ. Code art. 480). Each co-owner can make use of the thing and can dispose of his share of the thing. Co-ownership cannot be perpetual, in the sense that every co-owner has the right to get out of the indivision by demanding a partition either in kind or through a sale.

Ownership in the form of trust is a distinctive institution of Anglo-American common law . The Louisiana Trust Code defines trust as "the relationship resulting from the transfer of title to property to a person to be administered by him as a fiduciary [the trustee] for the benefit of another [the beneficiary]." For a civilian, the exact nature of this division between the fiduciary and the beneficiary is not clear. As long as the trust exists, only the fiduciary/trustee has the right to manage the thing and to dispose of it. At the end of the trust, the beneficiary will have the right to obtain the full and entire ownership of the thing that had been managed up to this point by the fiduciary/trustee.

The right of ownership can form the object of two types of dismemberments. These dismemberments fall out into one of two categories: servitudes and building restrictions. Servitudes themselves are of two kinds: the servitudes called "predial" (or "praedial"),which we would call "foncières," and the servitudes called "personal" which we would call "personnelles."

A servitude is predial (or foncière) when it consists of a charge imposed "on a servient estate for the benefit of a dominant estate" (La. Civ. Code art. 646). The charge may consist of an obligation not to do and,extraordinarily, of an obligation to do. A predial (foncière) servitude can be established by legislation or created by contract. An example of a predial servitude established by legislation is the right of passage that benefits one estate, called dominant, that is without a way of access because it is totally surrounded by another estate, called servient, which must give an access way to this dominant estate. By contract, the owners of two estates can create a servitude such as right of passage or a right of pasturage, for the benefit of the dominant estate of one owner on the servient estate of the other owner.

There are three forms of the servitudes that are called personal servitudes. In the first place, usufruct, in its two forms: usufruct of consumables and usufruct of nonconsumables. In principle, the duration of a usufruct is the duration of the life of the usufructuary. Another personal servitude is the right of use, which is a charge on a servient estate for the benefit of a person. The third personal servitude is the right of habitation which is the strictly personal right given to a person to inhabit the house of another person. It is defined as a "nontransferable real right to dwell in the house of another"(La. Civ. Code art. 630). Like usufruct, it terminates at the death of the beneficiary.

Servitudes under the form of building restrictions are of Anglo-Saxon origin. These restrictions are "charges imposed by the owner of an immovable in pursuance of a general plan governing building standards, specified uses, and improvements."(La. Civ. Code art. 775). "Building restrictions may be established only by juridical act executed by the owner of an immovable or by all the owners of the affected immovables." (La. Civ. Code art. 776). These charges, the Civil Code civil provides, are "likened to predial servitudes" in the sense that they benefit and burden estates.

The Louisiana Civil Code considers the possession of a thing to be a power over a thing as a matter of *fact* (Civ. Code art. 3422). Possession is "the detention or enjoyment of a corporeal thing, movable or immovable" with "the intent to possess that thing as owner."(La. Civ. Code arts 3421–3427). For incorporeals, Louisiana recognizes the concept of "quasi-possession." Possession is made of two elements, a material element, which is the detention of the thing, "*corpus*," and a psychological element, which is the intent to act like the owner (*animus domini*) of the thing. For possession to have legal effects, it is necessary that it be peaceable, continuous, and public.

Though possession is a situation of fact, it can, depending on the circumstances, produce legal effects. A possessor who has been in possession of a thing for a year, "acquires the right to possess it" (La. Civ. Code art.3422). He can prove his right by bringing a possessory action. Under some circumstances, the possessor can even become the owner of the thing.If a thing is movable and belongs to no one (a *res nullius*), the possessor becomes the owner of it the instant he takes possession of it. This mode of acquiring the right of ownership bears the name of "occupancy." If the thing is the property of someone other than the possessor, the latter can nevertheless acquire the ownership of it if he has the possession of it for a period of time, depending on whether he is in good faith or bad faith and depending on whether the thing was or was not acquired with a just title. This mode of acquiring ownership is known as "acquisitive prescription." The duration of the period of possession varies depending on whether the possessor is in good faith or not and depending on the immovable or movable nature of the thing. If the thing is immovable, the possessor must have the possession of it for ten years, must be in good faith, and must have a just title. In the contrary case, if he is in bad faith or without a just title, he must possess it for thirty years. In movable matters, the possession is of three years if the possession is in good faith and it is of ten years if he is in bad faith.

3. USE OF THINGS FOR PURPOSES OF SECURITY

Every thing can, in principle, serve to provide security for a debt or to be given as a guarantee for the performance of an obligation. Rights that are granted on such a thing are considered sometimes as accessory real rights, so as to distinguish them from principal real rights, and at other times as "real security," so as to distinguish them from personal security.

The most important and most general distinction is that which is made between conventional real security, on the one side, and legal real security, on the other. A second classification takes into consideration the nature of the thing, movable or immovable, on which the security bears. A third distinction turns on knowing whether, during the existence of the real security, the beneficiary of this security has obtained the possession of the thing or not. In the first case, one speaks of a possessory right, and in the second of a non-possessory rigth or right without possession.

Louisiana law knows only one kind of conventional immovable security: mortgage (hypothèque). Being a non-possessory right of real security, a conventional mortgage must be established by writing and has effect in regard to third persons only if it has been inscribed in the public records (mortgage records).

With respect to conventional movable security, the situation is relatively complex. Louisiana law recognizes two such sorts of movable real security: pledge, which is of Romano-Germanic origin, and security interest, which is of Anglo-Saxon origin, in particular, and is derived from Article 9 of the Uniform Commercial Code. Today the scope of application of security interests is so vast that pledge rarely finds any application. To be opposable to third persons and to bind the parties, a pledge must be made in written form. A security interest requires that the grantor sign a written document called a "security agreement," containing a description of the movable thing on which the security interest bears. In addition, to have legal effects against third persons, the security interest must form the object of a "financing statement" that will be registered in a special registry designed for this type of security.

One must also mention privileges, which can be general or special. They are general when they bear on all of the things, immovables and movables, that the debtor possesses. They are special when they bear on a particular thing, immovable or movable, of the debtor. An example of a general privilege is that of the "expenses of last illness" which is accorded to doctors and other caregivers, and bears on the entire estate of the deceased (La. Civ. Code Art. 3252). An example of a special privilege is that of the vendor, which bears only on the very thing sold to guarantee to the seller the payment of the purchase price by the buyer (La. Civ. Code Art. 3217-7). These privileges are created by legislation and, as a result, are not subjected to any requirements of publicity.

If the debtor does not perform the obligation as to which the privilege exists, the privileged creditor may cause the thing to be seized and sold by judicial process to collect the price of the sale. In his relations with third persons, the privileged creditor will have the right of preference over the other creditors of the same debtor, which will permit him to be paid before the others. If each of several creditors has a special privilege on the same thing, the Civil Code the Civil Code has established a ranking system for these special privileges. According to the ranking system that applies to many privileges, the most ancient will be the first served.

4. DISPOSITION OF THINGS

The owner of a right of ownership or of any real right on a thing other than the right of ownership is, in principle, free to dispose of this thing as seems good to him and to the extent that it is agreeable to him. This principle, though it holds true for most dismemberments of ownership, is not applied to the right of habitation, which is strictly personal to the holder, may not be disposed of, nor to servitudes that affect servient and dominant estates.

The power of the holder of a real right to dispose freely of his right or thing may not, as a general rule, be restricted by contract or other juridical act. Thus, a clause of inalienablitiy will be considered inapplicable and nonexistent, save if it is limited in its duration and justified by a legal interest. Some exceptions to this general rule exist in the law of trusts. The creator or founder of a trust, the settlor, can stipulate that some beneficiary will not be able to dispose of his interest in the trust while the trust remains in existence. He can also stipulate that the thing placed in trust cannot be alienated while the trust remains in existence. Nevertheless, if the thing is an immovable, a stipulation of this nature will cease to be applicable after a certain time has passed.

The modes of alienation of the right of ownership are multiple. The alienation can be by onerous title, such as sale, exchange, or dation en paiement, or by gratuitous title such as a donation. An alienation of the right of ownership can be *inter vivos* (a sale or a donation inter vivos) or *mortis causa* (an intestate succession or legacy).

The form with which an alienation of the right of ownership of a thing may or must be clothed varies with the juridical nature of the alienation and the nature of the thing that is alienated. If the alienation is *mortis causa*, it must necessarily be made in the form of a testament (either olographic or notarial: La. Civ. Code Arts 1575, 1576). If it is *inter vivos*, then the form will vary according to whether it is movable or immovable. In the second case, the alienation must be made in written form, an authentic act or an act under private signature, so that it can be recorded, which will render the alienation opposable to third parties. If the thing is a movable thing, then depending on whether the "cause" of the alienation is onerous or gratuitous, a simple exchange of consent may suffice or a form may be required. A writing in authentic form is required if the thing is an incorporeal thing and the cause of the alienation is gratuitous. If the thing is movable and corporeal, the exchange of consent by the parties will produce effects between the parties, but delivery of the thing will be necessary for the alienation to take effect against third persons.

Bibliography

Louisiana Pocket Civil Code, 2018 Edition, Carolina Academic Press.

J.Randall Trahan, Louisiana Law of Property: A Précis (Carolina Academic Press 2012).

Dictionary of the Civil Code, Alain Levasseur, Marie-Eugénie Laporte-Legeais, Juriscope, (LexisNexis 2014).

CHAPTER NINE

CONTRACT

Title 3 of Book III of the Louisiana Civil Code is entitled "Of Obligations in General." This Title comprises six chapters from "General Principles" (Chapter 1) to the "Extinction of Obligations" (Chapter 6). A good knowledge and understanding of these chapters are absolutely necessary so as to acquire the basic foundation for the study of Obligations in general and, therefore, for the study of Title 4, "Of Conventional Obligations or Contracts." In this study of Contract in Louisiana law, however, we cannot treat the various "Kinds of Obligations" that are covered in Title 3 (personal, heritable, conditional, subject to a term, solidary, joint, conjunctive, alternative, indivisible, etc.), nor the transfer of obligations (through assumption or subrogation, etc.), nor the modes of extinction of obligations (impossibility of performance, novation, remission of debt, confusion).

We will, however, select two articles in Chapter 1 of Title 3 on "General Principles" that apply particularly to contract and that provide a foundation for numerous rules framing the legal regime of contract generally and especially the performance of contracts.

Article 1756 defines an obligation as follows: *"An obligation is a legal relationship whereby a person, called the obligor, is bound to render a performance in favor of another, called the obligee. Performance may consist of giving, doing, or not doing something."* Article 1759, in turn, announces the fundamental principle of good faith that governs all obligations and conventional obligations in particular: *"Good faith shall govern the conduct of the obligor and the obligee in whatever pertains to the obligation."* The inclusion of this article among the general principles that govern Obligations in general is the solemn expression of the will of the legislator (La. Civ. Code arts. 1 & 2), to the effect that parties to an obligation must conform themselves to moral, social and economic purposes that transcend their individual interests. Courts also must effectuate this principle when ruling on the creation and performance of conventional obligations for which the foundations are freedom of contract and the autonomy of consent or "*consensualisme.*"

1. CONTRACT IN PRIVATE LAW

Articles 1907 to 1917 lay out the general principles of contract in Title IV. They define the different types of contract (unilateral or bilateral, onerous or gratuitous, etc.), all of which derive from the key definition of contract in Article 1906: *"A contract is an agreement by two or more parties whereby obligations are created, modified, or extinguished."*

1.1 FORMATION

Chapters 2 through 7 of Title IV impose four fundamental elements for the formation of a contract: capacity of each party; their consent; the existence of a cause; and the existence of an object.

As for the **capacity** of the parties, Article 1918 states the principle: *"All persons have capacity to contract, except unemancipated minors, interdicts, and persons deprived of reason at the time of contracting."* This article is an application to contracts of the rule stated in Article 27: "*all natural persons enjoy general legal capacity to have rights and duties.*" Therefore, a contract made by a person without legal capacity will be relatively null. For further details of the rules governing capacity, we refer the reader to the chapters of this work on persons.

As regards consent, Article 1927 states: "*A contract is formed by the **consent** of the parties established through offer and acceptance.*"

Negotiations that preceded the contract are governed by the general principle of good faith as required by Article 1759. An offer or a unilateral promise, for example an option, binds the maker of this unilateral offer for a certain time. This offer must be sufficiently precise, firm, and serious so that its acceptance will form a contract. One may make an offer to one or to more than one identified persons, or indeed to the public at large as is the case of an offer of a reward. The duration of an offer may be irrevocable or revocable. If the offer states a certain time within which it must be accepted, then the offer is irrevocable for that time. If the offeror granted the offeree an unspecified time within which to accept, the offer is irrevocable for a reasonable time, after which the offer becomes revocable.

In order to form a contract, the acceptance must conform to the offer and must be communicated to the offeror either orally, in writing, or by action or inaction. In particular circumstances, the silence of the offeree may permit the offeror to consider that the offeree has accepted the offer. In addition, to begin to perform or to end a performance may amount to forms of acceptance.

If an offer is revocable, the offeree's transmission of acceptance forms the contract. If an offer is irrevocable, however, the contract is formed when the offeror receives the offeree's acceptance.

Error vitiates consent when it is as to a **cause** without which the obligation could not exist and this cause was known by the other party. Thus error may be as to the nature of the contract, the thing that is the object of the contract, or any circumstance that ought to have been taken into account in good faith. The party who obtains the annulment of the contract because of his own error may be liable for the loss suffered by the other party unless the latter ought to have known of the error.

Fraud is the second vice of consent. A comment in the La. Civ. Code suggests (wrongly) that fraud here is the equivalent of "*dol*" in French law or *dolus* in Roman law. There is no nullity unless fraud causes an error. If the victim of the fraud succeeds in annulling the contract, the court may also award damages and attorney fees.

Duress is the third vice of consent. The victim must have a reasonable fear of an unjust and considerable injury caused by the other party's violence or threat of violence. As with fraud, the court may award the victim of duress damages and attorney fees in addition to an annulment of the contract. On the other hand, if the threat is to carry out a lawful act or to exercise a right, there is no duress.

Lesion as a vice of consent is mentioned but once in Title IV, limiting its range to cases provided by law, namely: sale and partition of successions.

In 1984, after much debate, the Louisiana legislature decided to keep **cause** as an essential element in the formation and the existence of a contract. Article 1966 of the Civil Code is explicit: "*An obligation cannot exist without a lawful cause,*" and "*cause is the reason why a party obligates himself*" (La. Civ. Code Art.1967). Also in 1984, and under the influence of the Anglo-American common law, the Civil Code introduced detrimental reliance in the definition of cause: "*A party may be obligated by a promise when he knew or should have known that the promise would induce the other party to rely on it to his detriment and the other party was reasonable in so relying. Recovery may be limited to the expenses incurred or the damages suffered as a result of the promisee's reliance on the promise. Reliance on a gratuitous promise made without required formalities is not reasonable.*" (La. Civ. Code Art. 1967 ¶2.)

As regards the **object** of a contract, it may be any lawful thing, possible, present or future, determined or determinable. The quantity of the object must be determined or determinable, but nothing is said about its quality in the chapter on "Object and Matter of Contracts." But when the obligor must perform by giving a thing, he need not give a thing of the best quality, nor may he give a thing of the worst (La. Civ. Code art.1860).

Article 1977 provides that a contract may have as its object a certain performance (or commitment to perform) by a third person, an original contribution in the Louisiana code. This institution is still known by its French name, the *promesse de* ***porte-fort*** .The party who promises that a third party will perform or commit will himself be liable in damages if the promised performance or commitment does not occur.

Likewise, a stipulation for the benefit of a third party (La. Civ. Code Art. 1978) may be the object of a contract. Here again, the institution is often recognized by its French name, ***stipulation pour*** **autrui**. A party to a contract may, as part of that contract, stipulate (hence, the stipulator) a benefit that the other contracting party must promise (hence, the promisor) to provide for a third party (hence, the third-party beneficiary). The third-party beneficiary may demand performance by the stipulator and the stipulator may demand performance by the promisor.

In general, the Civil Code adheres to the principle of "consensualism" or party autonomy, yet the Code requires, here and there, a formality under the form either of an act under private signature or of an authentic act (in particular for transactions in immovables), or still a real transfer of a thing (as in the contract of loan).

If one of the conditions for the formation of a contract fails to exist, the contract is null. The nullity will be relative if the absent condition is designed to protect the private interest of a party; it will be absolute if the condition protects public order.

1.2 PERFORMANCE

Article 1983 of the Civil Code declares the obligatory force of contracts as a fundamental principle: contract have an effect equivalent to a law for the parties and may only be dissolved by their consent or for reasons provided by law. And contracts must be performed in good faith, as stated as a matter of general principle in Article 1759.

A contract between two parties may produce benefits for third parties in cases specially provided for by law, such as third-party beneficiary contracts in Article 1978. By the same token, a contract may transfer or assign rights and obligations to heirs or particular assignees.

Because of the principle of the relative effect of contracts, a contract may have no effect "against" third parties in the sense that a contract cannot be contrary to their interests. Here one must mention simulation, which is a contract that does not express the true intentions of the parties, whereas the counter-letter does express the true intentions of parties to a simulation. Because third persons are unaware of the contents of the counter-letter, it can have no effect against third persons in good faith.

If an obligor fails to perform an obligation either not to do something, or to deliver a thing, or to sign an act, the court may order the obligor to perform that very act (specific performance). Furthermore, if the obligor's performance is late, the court may order payment of damages for the harm caused by the delay. Such damages for delaying a performance are called "moratory damages."

Nevertheless, if the court finds that specific performance would be unreasonable in the circumstances, it may substitute an award of money damages. In case of failure to perform an obligation to do, the court has the discretion to order damages or to grant specific performance.

Upon the request of the obligee or the decision of the court, the court may order an obligor who fails to perform at all or who performs poorly or late to pay compensatory damages. The parties may not include in their contract a clause that excludes or limits the liability of a party for intentional or gross fault that causes harm to the other party.

The court sets the amount of damages based on two criteria. First, damages are based on the **loss** the obligee sustained and the **profit** the obligee did not realize because of the failure to perform (La. Civ. Code art. 1995: loss sustained plus profit deprived). One goal the courts pursue here is the extinction of certain reciprocal obligations through "compensation."(La. Civ. Code Art. 1894.) The second criterion is good faith in the performance of a contract. If the obligor fails to perform but he is in good faith, he owes only damages for a harm that, at the time of formation of the contract, was a reasonably foreseeable result of the failure to perform. If, however, the obligor fails to perform and is in bad faith, he owes all damages that are the direct result of the failure to perform, foreseeable or unforeseeable.

The obligee as well is governed by good faith when the contract is formed and when it is performed. Thus, if the obligee concealed or disguised facts he knew or ought to have known would lead to the obligor's failure to perform, then the obligee may not recover damages when the obligor does fail to perform. Moreover, the obligee must act to mitigate or reduce the harm caused by the obligor's failure to perform. If the obligee does not act to mitigate, his damages will be correspondingly reduced.

The obligee may also seek recovery of damages for late performance as such (moratory damages). If the obligor's performance was subject to a determined or determinable term, the arrival of that term puts the obligor in default automatically. If the contract is synallagmatic, the obligor may plead that the other party has failed to perform (*exceptio non adimpleti contractus*), which permits the obligor to suspend performance of his own obligation for so long as the other party cannot or does not perform his own obligation. (La. Civ. Code art. 1993.)

If the obligor fails to perform his obligation, the obligee may seek the dissolution of the contract. (La. Civ. Code art. 2013.) Moreover, if one party fails to perform, the other may put him in default and may consider the contract dissolved unless the obligor performs within the agreed time. Article 2013 also provides that depending on the circumstances the obligee may deem the contract dissolved.

The dissolution of a contract does not affect the rights that third parties acquire in good faith and onerously. If the contract involves an immovable, the rules on recordation apply, which determine whether the transferee or possessor of an interest in an immovable prevails.

Articles 2036 through 2043 govern the revocatory or Paulian action, which gives the obligee the right to annul his obligor's act or the result of his obligor's failure to act, provided either event occurs after the right of the obligee arises and either event causes or aggravates the obligor's insolvency. As for the oblique action, Article 2044 give it a definition that is difficult to distinguish from the revocatory action, and the jurisprudence has yet to implement it.

2. ASPECTS OF GOVERNMENT CONTRACTS

The adjective "**administrative**" does not have the same meaning in Louisiana as it does in French administrative law. Every contract with the state of Louisiana or with any of its many agencies is theoretically governed by the conditions on formation of contracts set out in the Civil Code. Nevertheless, the most important provisions of such contracts are imposed unilaterally by a governmental agency as a function of its fields of activity and of its duty of "neutrality." Thus these agencies, like any private employer, are bound to follow numerous laws that protect their employees. This is the case, for example, under the laws that forbid discrimination by age, physical condition, religion, race, etc.

The economic and financial importance of **construction** contracts means that they are submitted to very detailed regulations, as shown by the length alone of Title 38 of the Louisiana Revised Statutes, entitled "Public Contracts, Works and Improvements" (La. Rev. Stat. 38:1 to 38:3381) and of Title 39 (La. Rev. Stat. 39:1 to 38:2192), the latter just as important, as it deals with the finances of the State and of all its political and administrative subdivisions.

In Louisiana, what is called a "public law contract" derives from a unique domain of the law that evolved over many years in order to establish rules and procedures to assure the maximum possible equality and transparency among the firms invited to submit bids in response to the announcement of a request for bids and proposals by a government agency.

Bibliography

Louisiana Pocket Civil Code, 2018 Edition, Carolina Academic Press

Levasseur A., Louisiana Law of Obligations in General, 4th ed. 2015, Carolina Academic Press.

Levasseur A., Louisiana Law of Conventional Obligations, 2nd ed. 2015, Carolina Academic Press.

CHAPTER TEN

DELICTUAL LIABILITY

The primary source of delictual responsibility in Louisiana is La. Civ. Code art. 2315 providing that "[e]very act whatever of man that causes damage to another obliges him by whose fault it happened to repair it." The concept of "fault" includes intentional fault, negligence, and strict liability. Louisiana courts have relied on article 2315 to read much of the common law of torts into Louisiana law.

Intentional torts include battery, assault, false imprisonment, trespass to land, conversion and trespass to chattels.[1] Louisiana frequently uses labels that are more consistent with the Louisiana Civil Code ("intentional interference with immovables" rather than "trespass") but the application is almost always consistent with the common law counterparts. One notable exception involves a line of cases that distinguishes "common law conversion" from "civilian conversion," but recent caselaw confirms that Louisiana conversion is identical with common law conversion.

Intent is purpose or substantial certainty, and it is clear that no evil intent is necessary. Rather, to use battery as an example, the only intent required is purpose or substantial certainty of prohibited contact. Although there continue to be a number of interesting

1. There are other intentional torts, such as defamation or spoliation, which are not discussed.

cases, intentional torts are important in Louisiana primarily to create an exception to the workplace immunity afforded to employers.

In contrast to intentional torts, negligence is the most important and most prevalent tort in Louisiana. The Louisiana approach to negligence is what courts have called the "familiar" duty-risk approach. The duty-risk approach requires the plaintiff to prove five elements: cause-in-fact, duty, breach, scope of the risk, and injury.

The "cause-in-fact" element requires the plaintiff to prove, more probably than not, that the alleged negligent act was the "but for" cause of the injury. If the injury would not have occurred in the absence of the negligent act, then the "but for" element is met. In rare circumstances involving multiple, independent, sufficient causes, the court may apply a "substantial factor" test of causation, finding the cause-in-fact element satisfied when the alleged negligent act was a "substantial factor" in producing the harm. However, the substantial factor test is poorly developed and most Louisiana cases are resolved by applying the "but for" test.

Louisiana courts have considered other methods of proving causation, such as "market-share" liability, imposing liability jointly on a group of defendants whose products or conduct created uniform risks, and allocating liability based on the market-share of the defendants. These alternate tests for causation have been universally rejected in Louisiana as deviating too far from the traditional "but for" test.

"Duty," the second element of Louisiana negligence, requires the defendant to exhibit the level of care of an ordinary, reasonable, prudent person in similar circumstances. In many cases, such as a typical car accident, a lay jury may be able to determine how reasonable, ordinary people should behave. However, the party may present evidence of reasonable conduct. Even the most mundane negligence cases typically involve expert witnesses. Indeed, in certain torts cases such as medical malpractice, expert testimony concerning reasonable care is a de facto requirement. In addition, parties may present evidence of customary behavior, national safety standards, internal company policy, etc... to establish that the conduct was either reasonable or unreasonable. Similarly, the doctrine of negligence per se admits non-tort statutes, usually criminal statutes, as "some evidence" of how reasonable ordinary people behave. In order to be admissible, the plaintiff must be within the class of persons the statute protects, and the risk must be within the class of risks the statute prevents. While some states will presume or even require a finding of unreasonable conduct where the defendant violates the statute, Louisiana treats the statutory violation as some evidence of negligence. In rare cases, where the injury would not have occurred in the absence of negligence, courts may instruct the jury on the doctrine of *res ipsa loquitur*, or the thing speaks for itself, allowing the factfinder to infer negligence in the absence of specific evidence of negligence. However, recent caselaw restricts the use of *res ipsa loquitur* to cases meeting a very stringent test. As a result, *res ipsa loquitur* is rare in Louisiana negligence cases.

Perhaps the most important measure of the reasonableness of defendant's conduct is the "risk-utility balance" as embodied in the Hand Formula. The risk-utility formula finds conduct to be unreasonable when the burden (broadly defined) of the untaken precaution is less than the loss discounted by the probability associated with the untaken precaution.

The "breach" element is typically the most straightforward of the duty-risk elements. If the defendant met the duty, there is no breach. If the defendant did not fulfill the duty, then the breach element is satisfied. However, the Louisiana Supreme Court recently tried to complicate the issue by suggesting that the "risk-utility balance" should apply at the breach element rather than the duty element. The resolution of this issue is important because duty is traditionally an issue of law decided by the judge, while breach is a factual question more likely decided by a jury. After addressing the issue at least three times in four years, the Louisiana Supreme Court decided to leave the risk-utility balance as a question of duty, and simplify the breach analysis once again.

"Scope of the risk" (or scope of the duty) is perhaps the most uncertain of the negligence elements. The scope inquiry asks whether this defendant *should* be responsible to this plaintiff for this injury that occurred in this way. Like their common law counterparts, Louisiana courts usually resolve this issue by examining whether the injury to this plaintiff was a reasonably foreseeable result of the defendant's negligence. However, Louisiana explicitly includes other factors in the analysis. For example, Louisiana courts may apply the "ease association" test, asking whether the injury to this plaintiff is one of the risks that would lead us to conclude that the defendant behaved unreasonably, or whether this risk is too remote to impose liability. Similarly, Louisiana courts have considered that policy factors (known as the *Pitre* policy factors) may be useful. The *Pitre* policy factors include the need for compensation, the need for deterrence, efficient administration of law, and other similar considerations. In *Pitre v. Opelousas General Hospital*, 530 So. 2d 1151 (1988), the case announcing the *Pitre* policy factors, Justice Dennis specifically incorporates the common law approach into a similar analysis under the Louisiana Civil Code, resulting in the hybrid analysis discussed here. The overwhelming majority of cases are resolved through foreseeability alone.

For the "injury" element, most relevant cases involve clear damage to property or person. However, there are a couple of interesting questions. First, Louisiana has addressed the issue of whether a plaintiff who views an injury to another and suffers only emotional injury may recover. La. Civ. Code art. 2315.6 provides that a limited set of family members may recover when: (1) they come upon the scene soon after the initial negligence, (2) the injured person suffers the type of injury that can reasonably be foreseen as causing emotional injury to the plaintiff, and (3) the emotional distress is severe.

Another interesting issue relating to the injury element deals with malpractice or professional negligence. Louisiana has recognized that a "lost chance of survival" is a compensable damage in a medical malpractice case. Lost chance is applicable to situations where a patient loses a less than fifty percent chance of survival, and ultimately dies. Application of the "but for" standard would result in a finding of no causation. However, Louisiana recognizes that the damage is actually the lost chance, rather than the death itself. "But for" the negligent treatment, the plaintiff/patient would not have suffered the lost chance of survival. Thus, all elements of the tort of negligence are satisfied and the jury will assign a value to the lost chance damage. This damage is limited to the lost chance of survival in medical malpractice cases and does not apply to other types of cases.

The concept of fault in La. Civ. Code art. 2315 encompasses more than negligence. In the series of articles immediately following 2315, the Louisiana Civil Code once embodied a concept of strict liability. Liability is strict in the sense that it does not depend on proof of the personal negligence of the defendant. In a typical negligence case, the plaintiff must prove that the defendant knew, or through the exercise of reasonable care should have known, of the risk and failed to take reasonable care. The proper standard for determining strict liability is to presume the owner's knowledge of the risk of the thing under his control and then to determine the reasonableness (according to traditional notions of blameworthiness) of the owner's conduct in light of that presumed knowledge. To illustrate, assume that a tree owned by the defendant falls on the plaintiff's automobile causing damage. Further, assume that the tree appeared healthy and no reasonable person would have engaged in additional examination of the tree. Finally, assume that the tree was, in fact, rotten to the core. If the standard of liability is negligence, then the owner of the tree could escape liability by arguing that his conduct was reasonable because he neither knew, nor through the exercise of reasonable care should have known, that the tree was rotten. In contrast, if the theory of liability is strict liability, we presume that the owner knew the tree was rotten, meaning that the failure to take precautions (removing the tree) created an unreasonable risk of harm. In this way, the only difference between negligence and strict liability is that strict liability presumes knowledge of the risk. However, this presumption has very important implications for liability.

Prior to 1996, strict liability (or some version of strict liability) applied to those having custody of things (La. Civ. Code art. 2317), of persons such as a curator of an insane (La. Civ. Code art. 2319), or owners of animals (La. Civ. Code art 2321), and owners of buildings (La. Civ. Code art 2322). In 1996, the legislature amended many of these provisions by providing that the owner/custodian would be liable only upon a showing that: (1) the defendant knew or reasonably should have known of the vice or defect or condition that caused the harm, (2) the damage could have been prevented through the exercise of reasonable care, and (3) the defendant failed to exercise reasonable care. The intent of the legislature, as recognized by the courts, is to shift from strict liability to negligence. After amendment, strict liability applies only in cases against the owners of dogs and in certain types of product liability actions.[2]

The Louisiana Civil Code creates a third form of liability known as absolute liability or, more descriptively, liability without fault. The basis for this liability are the vicinage articles located at La. Civ. Code art. 667–669. Prior to 1996, these "obligations of neighborhood," were interpreted in a variety of ways. Many common law jurisdictions utilize a factor-based test and impose strict liability whenever the activity involves well-known, inherent and unavoidable risks. The standard also involves questions of whether the activity is suitable for the neighborhood. This common law test is very vague and applied very inconsistently. At various times in jurisprudential history, Louisiana courts have applied a test similar to the common law based factors, suggested that any liability in Louisiana is based solely on the Code, or applied a test that mixes the Code with the common law without identifying the source of the law. In 1996, the legislature simplified the analysis by amending La. Civ. Code art. 667 to provide that the only activities subjected to absolute liability are pile-driving and blasting. For all other activities, the standard of liability will be negligence.

2. Product Liability is discussed in more depth later.

In addition to the Civil Code, there are several important statutes that create or clarify tort liability. Two of the more important statutes are the Louisiana Product Liability Act (LPLA) and the Medical Malpractice Act (MMA). The LPLA provides the exclusive theory of recovery for plaintiffs seeking to recover tort damages from the manufacturers of products. Unlike many common law jurisdictions that struggle with the definition of "defect" and various standards of liability, the LPLA creates relatively clear standards. The statute requires the plaintiff to prove that the defendant is a manufacturer of a defective product that causes damage while the product is used in a reasonably anticipated way. The statute further limits defect to four specific categories: defects in construction or composition, design defects, unreasonable failure to warn, or breach of an express warranty. The construction or composition claim is that the product is defective because it fails to live up to the manufacturer's own specifications and deviates from other products from the same manufacturer. The standard is strict liability in the sense that we presume that the manufacturer knew of the risk of this particular product. The classic example is the Coke bottle that explodes without explanation. It may be the only Coke bottle of 100,000 that explodes, but we presume that the manufacturer knew of the weakness in the particular bottle, making it quite likely that the manufacturer is liable. Most LPLA cases are either design defect cases or failure to warn cases. A product is defective in design when there is an alternative design available that could have prevented the harm and the burden of adopting the alternate design is less than the loss associated with the actual design discounted by the risk of that design. The LPLA requires that the plaintiff provide evidence of a risk utility balance comparing the actual design with the alternative design. Thus, the plaintiff must present statistical evidence of the number of similar incidents and the availability and feasibility of an alternative design. If the defendant can establish that the design utilized the state of the art in safety technology at the time of production, then there is no liability. A product is defective for a failure to warn when a manufacturer fails to provide a warning that would have prevented the harm. However, the plaintiff must still present some evidence of the risk associated with the product. The manufacturer need not warn of obvious risks or minimal risks or risks that it neither knew, nor reasonably should have known, were associated with its product. Breach of express warranty cases are rare because the manufacturer must make an express warranty.

The reasonably anticipated use definition includes some reasonably anticipated misuses, but the concept has created some uncertainty among courts and scholars. For example, one case held that shooting a gun with part of the locking mechanism removed was not a reasonably anticipated use, while a dissent argued that it was clearly a use and that the question was whether the design unreasonably created the risk of firing the weapon with part of the mechanism removed. The issue is highlighted here to point out that although the LPLA provides more certainty than the common law alternative, there is room for varying interpretations.

The Medical Malpractice Act clarifies the negligence standard as it applies to the medical profession. The MMA was a response to a perceived medical care crisis. The MMA recognizes two types of theories. A mistake in diagnosis or treatment is treated like any negligence case with the standard of care or duty determined by the conduct of a duly licensed professional in the same or similar community. The second theory, called informed consent, requires that the health care professional disclose material risks involved in treatment alternatives, including the no treatment alternative. If the undisclosed risk then materializes, the patient will have an action for a failure of informed consent that proceeds like a negligence case. The MMA's most important and controversial provisions relate to damages and procedure. The MMA requires that all medical malpractice cases proceed to a Medical Review Panel (MRP) prior to a trial in court. The MRP consists of three licensed healthcare professionals who will render their opinion concerning whether the defendant breached the standard of care or not. The result of the MRP is not binding and either party may then proceed to trial with the MRP opinion admitted as an expert report. However, the parties may contest the MRP opinion and present other experts that contradict the findings of the MRP, and the factfinder may reach a result that is contrary to the MRP conclusion. Another procedural aspect of the MMA involves the source of any damage payment. All Qualified Healthcare Professionals (QHCPs) must provide evidence of $100,000 of private malpractice insurance. In addition, the QHCPs pay fees to the state government. These fees are accurately characterized as premiums by many commentators. The QHCP will then be responsible for the $100,000 of liability, with any remainder paid by a governmental agency known as the Patient Compensation Fund (PCF). In addition, the maximum amount that any plaintiff may recover is $500,000, exclusive of future medical costs. The cap on damages in medical malpractice action has been very controversial, but remains a fixture of medical malpractice in Louisiana.

Defendants have many immunities and defenses available. For example there are immunities for the organizers of parades, owners of land used for recreational purposes, and those engaged in charitable activities. Workers recover from their employers or co-employees for job-related injuries through an administrative system known as Workers Compensation, but the employer is immune from lawsuits. Although the state and local governments have waived immunity in the state constitution, there are complex procedures involved in suing and collecting judgments from governmental entities and the maximum liability is $500,000.

The most common defense is the defense of comparative fault. In La. Civ. Code arts. 2323 & 2324, Louisiana has combined the defenses of comparative fault (reduction in recovery due to the plaintiff's own fault) and allocation of fault among defendants into a single inquiry. While there are a plethora of different combinations and variations for comparative fault, the Louisiana system is deceptively simple. All responsible parties, regardless of the theory of liability, are allocated a percentage of fault, and each party is responsible only for the allocated percentage. In addition, immune, judgment-proof or absent parties also receive an allocation of fault, even though the plaintiff will not be able to collect any judgment. Thus, with a few minor exceptions, Louisiana has eliminated solidary liability from tort law.

Determining the percentage of fault attributable to each party, including the plaintiff, is a fact issue and is performed by the jury with little guidance. However, courts provide juries with a list of factors that can guide the allocation. The factors include whether the conduct resulted from inadvertence or involved an awareness of the danger, how great a risk was created by the conduct, the significance of what was sought by the conduct, the capacities of the actor, whether superior or inferior, and any extenuating circumstances which might require the actor to proceed in haste.

Bibliography

Louisiana Pocket Civil Code, 2018 Edition, Carolina Academic Press
Maraist F., Louisiana Law of Torts, 2010, Carolina Academic Press

CHAPTER ELEVEN

QUASI-CONTRACTS

Until 1996, the Louisiana Civil Code dealt with quasi-contracts under Title V of Book III, entitled "Of Quasi Contracts, and of Offenses and Quasi Offenses." Article 2293 stated as a definition that: "Quasi contracts are the lawful and purely voluntary act of a man, from which there results any obligation whatever to a third person, and sometimes a reciprocal obligation between the parties." Two sections followed, one on the management of another's affairs, the other on the payment of a thing not due.

In 1996, this Title V was completely rewritten and is now entitled: "Obligations Created without Agreement." Articles 2292 to 2305 deal with the management of (another's) affairs, enrichment without cause, and payment of a thing not owed. If the definition and the concept of quasi-contract have disappeared from today's Civil Code, the concept of quasi-contract as understood in Anglo-American common law continues to influence the Louisiana jurisprudence. Therefore one ought to analyze the concept as understood in the common law first before turning to articles 2292 to 2305 of the Civil Code.

In the common law a so-called quasi contract is of two distinct types. First, it is a contract implied in law, that is, a contract that the law deems to have been created despite the absence of any manifestation of consent either express or tacit, expressed orally or by action. The second type of quasi contract is the contract implied in fact, which is a contract whose existence is the outcome of acts that stand for the implicit consent of the parties. Thus, a contract implied in fact is truly a contract formed by consent of the parties, while a contact implied in law is not.

Common-law courts are little troubled by this important difference in the source of an obligation, whether that source be in the law or in the parties themselves. Still the different effects of these two forms of quasi contract should distinguish them. For contracts implied in law, one party owes the other restitution, whereas contracts implied in fact create a contractual obligation that must be performed, often bilaterally. Finally, one must recognize that a contract implied in law, *for a civilian*, is simply not a contract at all. It is precisely the enrichment of one party that causes the law to impose an obligation of restitution toward the party impoverished. The two typical fact patterns for contracts implied in law are *quantum meruit*, in cases of services provided, and *quantum valebat/valebant*, in the case of sale.

Louisiana courts freely borrowed these two types of quasi contracts from the common law where one party provided services or delivered a thing to another. In so doing, Louisiana courts distorted the concept of an implied in law contract by using it for situations which Louisiana law otherwise would have characterized as simply contractual in nature.

Thus, Louisiana's three kinds of "obligations that arise without agreement" in Title V of Book III are of an entirely different nature. These obligations arising without agreement or consent are (1) the management of affairs, (2) enrichment without cause, and (3) payment of a thing not owed.

The **management of affairs**, also known by its Latin name, *negotiorum gestio,* is regulated by articles 2292 to 2297. This situation occurs when one person, the manager, undertakes on his own initiative, without having received the power to protect the interests of another person, the owner, to act under the reasonable belief that if the owner knew of the circumstances he would approve the acts of the manager. It is unnecessary that the manager know the identity of the owner whose affair he manages. It is enough that the manager act with an altruistic intention to protect and preserve the interests of another person. By application of the rules of mandate by analogy, the manager may act both in the interests of the owner and in his own interest. Whether the manager acts in the interests of the owner exclusively or for the owner and himself, the manager must act with the intention, the *animus obligandi*, to bind the owner whose affair he has managed. In the Louisiana jurisprudence, the *animus obligandi* dominates whether the intention of the manager is either wholly or only partially altruistic. In other words, the courts lean toward finding a management of affairs in order to grant an action to one party in order to be "equitable" when another party has been enriched at the expense of the first party. This position of the courts has two bases. First, it is easy to assimilate the management of affairs to the contract of mandate, whose rules are well-established. Second, before the reform of 1996 was enacted, the concept of enrichment without cause was not well understood by the courts. Today the Louisiana courts apply rather freely the requirement that the manager act with the intention to manage the affair of another when he begins to act, when the facts and circumstances would otherwise justify concluding that the parties had formed a tacit or implied contract. Furthermore, the courts graft a management of affairs onto an implied or tacit contract when the parties do not immediately manifest an intention to be bound. Here Louisiana courts often resort to *quantum meruit* and *quantum valebat*, as noted above, so that one person, the owner, will not be unjustly enriched at the expense of another person, the manager.

The management of affairs often imposes reciprocal obligations between the manager and the owner, and even obligations with respect to third persons. The manager is bound to exercise all the care of a prudent administrator and if he fails to do so he could be held liable. As for the owner for whom an affair has been well administered, he may be held bound, by court decision if need be, to perform the commitments made by the manager to third persons, and to reimburse the manager for useful and necessary expenditures he made during his administration of the affair. Much like the principal in a contract of mandate, the owner may ratify commitments made by the manager that were neither useful nor necessary. Without the owner's ratification in those circumstances, the manager may be bound by obligations he made to third persons by juridical acts. That would occur, of course, if the obligations were neither necessary nor useful to the owner, and also if the manager acted in his own name without advising the third person that he was acting as representative of the owner.

Chapter 2 of Title V of the Civil Code is entitled "**Enrichment without Cause,**" Section 1 of which is "General Principles," and Section 2 is "Payment of a Thing Not Owed."

Article 2298 is the sole article under Section 1, "General Principles." It provides that there is enrichment without cause when a person who has been enriched without cause to the detriment of another person is bound to compensate the latter. The expression "without cause" is used in this context to exclude any case in which the enrichment is the result of a valid juridical act or of the law. The action in question is subsidiary and may not be brought when the law gives a right to recover to the person impoverished or announces a contrary rule. The amount of compensation is the lesser of the amount by which one party is enriched and the amount by which the other party is impoverished. These amounts are calculated at the moment the action is brought or, based on the circumstances, the moment the judgment is granted.

Before 1996, the Civil Code had no article on enrichment without cause. In 1967, however, the Louisiana Supreme Court recognized that an enrichment might be unjustified. In the well-known decision *Minyard v. Curtis Products, Inc.*, 205 So.2d 422 (La. 1967), the court drew inspiration from French doctrine and jurisprudence and it adopted the five elements of the action *de in rem verso*: 1. an enrichment; 2. an impoverishment; 3. a direct relationship between those two elements; 4. an absence of "cause" or justification for either element; and 5. the absence of any other action, hence the subsidiary nature of this action. Since 1996, the courts of appeal and the Louisiana supreme court have not much relied on this action and have not fully analyzed each element. They mention the action *de in rem verso* along with *quantum meruit* if there is no express contract between the parties, simply to limit the right to compensation to the lower of the two amounts noted above. Courts do not often take the trouble to find and construct a tacit or implied contract between two parties, judging that a quasi-contract handles the problem quite adequately.

There is **payment of a thing not owed** when a person who has received a thing or a payment of money not owed to him is held to make restitution to the person from whom it was received. In the Civil Code and jurisprudence, the action in restitution of a payment not due (the expression *condictio indebiti* is rarely used) may be brought as soon as a payment is made or a thing is delivered when no corresponding obligation exists. There is also payment of a thing not owed when the obligation to pay or to deliver is subject to a suspensive condition under article 2301.

A person who believes himself to be a debtor and pays the debt of another may demand that the creditor repay it. Still, the payer may not recover the payment if the creditor, because of having been paid, has disposed of an instrument that evidenced the creditor's right or has released the real or personal security that secured his right. In that case, the payer who erred has recourse against the true debtor. Should the recipient of the payment not due be in bad faith, he will be bound to restore both the principal and its fruits and products. If the thing is immovable or a corporeal movable, the recipient must restore the thing itself if it still exists. If the thing has been damaged, destroyed, or cannot be restored, the recipient in good faith at the time of receipt must restore its value if the loss was caused by his fault. If the recipient was in bad faith at that time, he must restore its value even if the loss was not caused by his fault.

Finally, if the recipient in good faith has alienated the thing, he is only bound to restore what he "obtained from the alienation," but if in bad faith he must pay damages also.

Liberative prescription of the action to recover payment of a thing not owed is ten years, the general prescriptive period for personal actions (La. Civ. Code art. 3499).

Bibliography

Louisiana Pocket Civil Code, 2018 Edition, Carolina Academic Press

CHAPTER TWELVE

BUSINESS ENTITIES

1. FORMS OF BUSINESS ENTITIES

The simplest form of business "entity" or enterprise under Louisiana law is the proprietorship, also commonly referred to as sole proprietorship since the business by its nature has but one owner. The use of the term "entity" here is, in fact, inaccurate, since, in contrast to all other forms of business organization, there is no separation in legal personality between the business and the proprietor, i.e., the natural person who is its owner. Thus, the assets of the business are owned by the proprietor; the income (or losses) of the business are those of the proprietor and are reported on his individual tax return; the employees of the business are employees of the proprietor; and, perhaps most importantly, the proprietor has unlimited personal liability for all obligations arising out of the operation of the business, whether delictual or contractual, except to the extent that an obligee agrees by contract to limit the proprietor's liability.

It is of course very common for proprietorships to operate not under the name of the proprietor but rather under an assumed or "trade" name. Louisiana statutory law provides for the public registration of assumed business names with penalties for violations, but it appears that the statute is rarely if ever enforced.

If two or more persons operate a business as co-owners, then the default form of entity is the partnership (referred to in the comments to the Civil Code as an "ordinary" partnership, analogous to the general partnership under the common law). Article 2801 of the La. Civ. Code explicitly recognizes a partnership as a juridical person distinct from its partners. Partnerships are unique among the forms of fictitious business entities, however, in that no public filing is necessary for their creation; while the Code provides that partnerships are created by contract, it is likewise clear that the contract of partnership need not be in writing. It should be noted, however, that unlike the law in many common-law states, Article 2806 of the Code requires that the contract be in writing for a partnership to own immovable property.

That said, a formal written agreement is highly desirable, inasmuch as the Code rules governing partnerships are for the most part default, suppletory rules (except for those involving the rights of third parties). Thus, for example, in the absence of contrary agreement, partners share profits, losses, and assets equally, although capital contributions are restored according to contributions made (Article 2803); each partner is entitled to a single vote and ordinary business matters are decided by majority vote (Article 2807); and each partner is a mandatary of the partnership for all matters in the ordinary scope of its business except for transactions involving immovables (Article 2814). Obviously, all of those are matters as to which the parties could well desire a different regime, underscoring the importance of contracting out of the default rules.

One aspect of Louisiana partnership law that is essentially unique in the country is the personal liability of partners for obligations of the partnership. In other states, although the details may vary according to jurisdiction, partners generally have unlimited personal liability for partnership debts. In Louisiana, a partner is bound for only his "virile share" of partnership debts, which is construed as equal share counting by heads. (Article 2817). In contrast to the rule in several other states, the partnership itself is treated as the principal obligor; the partners are only secondarily liable for its debts.

It is, however, possible for an ordinary partnership to further limit the personal liability of its partners by electing to become a registered limited liability partnership, or RLLP (Revised Statutes Title 9, §§ 3431–3435). Notwithstanding the provisions of Civil Code Article 2817, a partner in such a partnership is not individually liable for liabilities and obligations of the partnership arising from errors, omissions, negligence, incompetence, malfeasance or willful or intentional misconduct committed by another partner or representative of the partnership. Of course, the election provides no protection against a partner's own acts or omissions. The election also does not limit a partner's liability for liabilities or obligations arising from any other cause (principally contracts); thus, practically the election of RLLP status is primarily beneficial in Louisiana for partnerships engaged in the practice of a profession. (It should be noted that in some states, the RLLP election protects partners from all partnership debts, not simply delictual ones.) The election requires annual filing with the Secretary of State together with a $125 filing fee. The partnership must include the words "registered limited liability partnership" or letters "L.L.P." in its name. The election does not create a different type of entity; it merely subjects an ordinary partnership to a special liability regime.

In turn, the registered limited liability partnership must be distinguished from the partnership in commendam or limited partnership (La. Civ. Code articles 2836–2844). Tracing its lineage to the twelfth century European "commenda," a partnership in commendam is composed of at least one general partner, who has the liability of a partner of an ordinary partnership, and at least one partner in commendam or limited partner, who has no liability beyond the loss of his investment in the partnership. In order to obtain that protection of partners in commendam, most importantly the contract of a partnership in commendam must be in writing and filed with the Secretary of State. It should be noted that the rule of absolute liability for nonfiling is also unique to Louisiana. Under the Uniform Limited Partnership Acts in effect in other states, there are no provisions for automatic loss of limited liability brought about by a failure to file, although all American limited partnership statutes in theory require a public filing. Also, the partnership's name must include language clearly identifying it as a partnership in commendam, such as the words "limited partnership" or "partnership in commendam"; and the name must not imply that a partner in commendam is a general partner. Partners in commendam are required to contribute to the partnership either money, things, or non-managerial services; the Civil Code comments state that a failure to do so also results in loss of limited liability.

Historically, there has been much uncertainty as to the extent that a partner in commendam could participate in the affairs of the partnership without risking the loss of limited liability. The traditional rule was that if a partner in commendam participated in the control of the business, he would be become liable as a general partner. That rule has, however, substantially eroded in recent years. Thus, Article 2844 has a non-exclusive list of "safe harbors" that are specifically excluded from "control" (e.g., being an agent or employee of the partnership, consulting with and advising a general partner, attending partnership meetings, voting on various matters, etc.). Moreover, regardless of the nature of a partner in commendam's participation, he is liable only to persons who do business with the partnership who reasonably believe, based on his conduct, that he is a general partner.

It should be noted that, due to the relatively recent introduction of limited liability companies to American Law (discussed below), it is now uncommon for start-up businesses to organize as partnerships in commendam.

A feature common to all partnerships is that they are not income tax paying entities. Rather, partnerships file only informational returns, and partners report income or losses on their own returns.

In Louisiana as in all other states, the only entity which, until the late twentieth century, offered limited liability to all owners of the entity is the corporation. Present Louisiana corporation law has relatively few distinctive features, since the Louisiana Business Corporation Act (Title 12, §§ 1-101 to 1-1703) is based on the American Bar Association's Model Business Corporation Act, which has been adopted by around two-thirds of American states. The statute therefore follows traditional structures: a corporation is formed by filing articles of incorporation with the Secretary of State; can have as few as one shareholder; is generally managed by a board of directors of one or more individuals, elected by the shareholders; and is operated by officers (which must include a secretary and can consist of such other officers whose titles are set by the bylaws or board) who are elected by the director(s). Corporations are, thus, in many ways enormously flexible; they can range from one shareholder, one director and one officer closely-held business to a publicly-traded business with hundreds of thousands of shareholders, scores of directors and hundreds of officers.

Shareholders are, of course, ordinarily insulated from personal liability for corporate debts. In closely-held corporations, however, courts believing that the corporation has been used to perpetrate fraud or inequitable conduct may "pierce the corporate veil" to impose liability on culpable shareholders.

A major potential drawback for corporations is that they are normally income tax paying entities. Thus arises the classic problem of "double taxation": the same income is taxed first to the corporation and then to its shareholders if they receive distributions which cannot be deducted by the corporation as an ordinary and necessary business expense (e.g., salary, rent or interest). Double taxation can be avoided for certain corporations with 100 or fewer shareholders by electing to be taxed under Subchapter S of the Internal Revenue Code, where taxation at the corporate level is eliminated.

Two provisions of the current Louisiana legislation diverge dramatically from traditional corporate law. First is the authorization in Section 1-732 of the Act for "unanimous governance agreements." This statute authorizes shareholders by unanimous written agreement (other than articles or bylaws) to make dramatic changes in ordinary corporate principles, e.g., eliminating or restricting the process of the board of directors; authorizing distributions disproportional to share ownership; authorizing dissolution of the corporation at a party's will; and so on.

The other innovative provision is the creation of a remedy for shareholder oppression as an alternative to an action seeking involuntary dissolution of the corporation. Under Section 1-1435, if a corporation engages in oppression of a shareholder, the shareholder may bring an action to withdraw from the corporation and require the corporation to buy all of the shareholder's shares at their judicially-determined fair value (if the parties cannot agree as to that). "Oppression" is considered to have occurred "if the corporation's distribution, compensation, governance and other practices, considered as a whole over an appropriate period of time, are plainly incompatible with a genuine effort on the part of the corporation to deal fairly and in good faith with the shareholder."

The final, and most recent form of entity recognized by Louisiana law is the limited liability company or LLC. The statutes authorizing LLCs, Title 12, §§ 1301–1369, were first enacted in 1992, part of a national phenomenon created by the decision of the Internal Revenue Service that LLCs would be taxed as partnerships for the purpose of federal income taxation. (That is now governed by the so-called IRS "Check-the-Box" regulations, which allow LLCs to elect whether to be taxed as partnerships or corporations; almost all chose partnership taxation.) LLCs are hybrids, with some features of corporations (e.g., limited liability of members) and some of partnerships (no taxation as an entity, flexible management structures and the like). Section 1303 thus states expressly that all limited liability companies have the powers, rights and privileges of both corporations and partnerships provided by Louisiana laws. It might be noted that, reflecting their partnership component, LLCs were originally required to have at least two members; that however was abandoned early on and it has long been permissible to form a single-member LLC.

LLCs are in one sense, like corporations, creatures of statute, since they can be formed only by filing articles of organization with the Secretary of State. At the same time, however, LLCs are like partnerships much more contract-oriented in general than corporations, since like the partnership articles in the Civil Code the Limited Liability Company Law incorporates a host of default rules which are subject to alteration either in the articles of organization or, more commonly, in a separate, private "operating agreement." Thus, for example, the default rule is that an LLC is managed by its members (similar to partnerships), each of whom is entitled to one vote (regardless of disproportionate financial interests) and who ordinarily act by majority vote. However, the articles of organization can provide for management by one or more managers, who may but need not be members (like corporate directors). Absent contrary provisions, managers likewise have a single vote and act by majority vote.

A striking, and potentially important, difference between partnerships and LLCs involves the rules on agency powers. As previously noted, under Civil Code Article 2814 all partners are deemed mandataries of the partnership for all matters in the ordinary course of business other than transactions involving immovables, and provisions to the contrary do not bind persons who in good faith transact business with such a partner. Under Section 1317 of the LLC Law, however, members or managers (depending on which election is made) have similar rights unless their powers are restricted, enlarged or eliminated by the articles of organization and a third person has knowledge of such provisions. Third parties are, however, deemed to have knowledge of such restrictions if contained in a written operating agreement and the articles contain a statement that such restrictions exist. Thus third persons are deemed to "know" of restrictions in a private document merely because of the reference in the publicly-filed articles, placing a possibly significant burden of inquiry on third persons.

While there are no formal restrictions on the size of an LLC's membership, practically they are limited by virtue of the default rule that the assignee of a member's interest does not become a member unless the other members unanimously consent in writing. Without that consent, the assignee only receives the right to whatever distributions to which the assignor was entitled. Thus LLCs are not adaptable to publicly-traded businesses.

2. DIFFICULTIES COMMON TO ENTERPRISES

All business enterprises are, of course, subject to the possibility of financial reverses. In those events, there are a variety of possible means by which creditors may be able to reach assets of the enterprise in order to satisfy the obligations owed to them. The most direct means of doing so is to obtain a mortgage (for immovable property) or security interest (for movable property) in specific assets owned by the business. In an event of default (as defined in the applicable credit agreement) occurring, then the creditor can initiate foreclosure proceedings to effect, typically, a sale of the collateral and the application of the proceeds of the sale to the secured debt. Depending upon the nature of the collateral, the sale may take place under judicial supervision or private act by the creditor. (It might be noted that Article 99 of the Uniform Commercial Code, or UCC, as adopted in many other states grants creditors broad rights to effect self-help repossession of corporeal movable collateral; as adopted in Louisiana, as part of the Louisiana Commercial Laws, the right of self-help under UCC Article 9 is severely restricted.)

In the absence of a formal grant of security, a creditor's main recourse is to obtain a judgment against the enterprise in a court of competent jurisdiction, and to then have assets of the enterprise seized through judicial process and liquidated in satisfaction of the judgment. It is important to note, however, that the rights of judgment creditors are generally inferior to those who hold a properly recorded mortgage or perfected security interest. Of course, a judgment creditor may also have conflicts with other creditors who enjoy statutory liens or privileges in the same property.

One of the most powerful tools (or at least bargaining chips) available to creditors is the commencement of an involuntary bankruptcy proceeding against the enterprise under either Chapter 7 (liquidation) or Chapter 11 (reorganization) of the Federal Bankruptcy Code. Although the grounds for involuntary relief are quite complex, in general if the debtor has 12 or more creditors, any three can commence such a case; if there are fewer than 12, only one is required. While involuntary cases represent only a very small percentage of bankruptcy filings, the specter of such a proceeding can allow creditors to bring enormous pressure against a debtor to settle on favorable terms.

By the same token, of course, the filing of a voluntary Chapter 11 reorganization case is an extremely common defensive mechanism for a debtor enterprise to keep creditors at bay. The automatic stay that goes into effect upon filing essentially brings all collection actions to a halt, while the debtor seeks to craft a judicially confirmable plan of reorganization. And, naturally, an enterprise which is prepared to concede financial defeat can simply file for voluntary liquidation under Chapter 7 of the Bankruptcy Code.

CHAPTER THIRTEEN

LABOR AND EMPLOYMENT LAW

1. INTRODUCTION

The labor and employment law of the United States is not a cohesive set of laws bound together by core principles. Instead, the principles manifested in statutes, regulations, and case law have developed over time in response to various issues and problems that have arisen. For example, the Fair Labor Standards Act, regulating minimum wage, overtime, and child labor, was part of President Franklin Roosevelt's New Deal legislation after the Great Depression. Title VII of the Civil Rights Act of 1964, which is the centerpiece of U.S. employment antidiscrimination law, was a product of the civil rights movement of the 1950s and 1960s.

In the 1930s, the paradigm of organized labor and collective bargaining and collective action prompted Congress to pass the Wagner Act (or National Labor Relations Act), which protected the rights of employees to join unions and engage in collective bargaining with their employers. Organized labor and collective bargaining reached its pinnacle in the 1950s and thereafter began a gradual decline that accelerated in the 1980s. Today, union density in the U.S. is very low—approximately 11 percent of the overall workforce and less than 7 percent of the private-sector workforce.

The 1960s marked a shift from laws based on collective action to development of individual employment rights law at both the federal and state levels. One type of individual employment rights law is antidiscrimination law. The 1960s through the early 1990s was a period in which antidiscrimination laws proliferated, beginning with Title VII of the Civil Rights Act of 1964 and culminating with the enactment of the Americans with Disabilities Act of 1990, the Civil Rights Act of 1991, the Genetic Information Nondiscrimination Act (GINA) of 2008, and the Americans with Disabilities Act Amendments Act of 2008. Other individual employment laws included labor standards legislation, such as the Family and Medical Leave Act of 1993. In addition to federal individual employment rights legislation, state legislatures passed laws, and state courts developed contract and tort theories to address employment disputes. Beginning around 2000, a theme of individual privacy in the workplace became a prominent concern in U.S. employment law. For example, many states passed laws regulating use of genetic information in employment and insurance decisions, and the federal government followed with the enactment of GINA in 2008.

Another feature of U.S. labor and employment law that is different from the law of many other nations is the interrelationship of health insurance and retirement plans and employment law. Although President Obama was successful in having national health care legislation enacted, the Patient Protection and Affordable Care Act of 2010 (often referred to as "Obamacare"), the future of that law and any replacement law is uncertain with the election of President Trump. It is sufficient to say that many U.S. citizens who work are dependent on employer-provided and partially subsidized health insurance. Furthermore, with the meager support available in retirement through the federal government's social security program, most citizens look for employer-provided and partially subsidized retirement benefits.

2. INDIVIDUAL EMPLOYMENT CONTRACTS: FORMATION AND TERMINATION

Employers and employees generally can agree in an employment contract to anything that is not illegal and not against public policy. Generally, most employees in the nation do not have individual employment contracts that vary the presumption of employment at will that pertains in 49 of the 50 states (Montana is the exception). Employment at will, although often called a doctrine, is essentially an evidentiary presumption that, absent evidence to the contrary, an employment relationship or contract does not include a good or just cause employment security provision, and the employment relationship is not for any specified duration. Thus, employment at will is a default rule: if employers and employees do not agree otherwise, employers can terminate employees at any time and for any reason. However, the reason for termination cannot be illegal. Illegal terminations include those based on race, sex, religion, age, national origin, disability, or any other characteristic covered by federal, state, or local antidiscrimination laws. Employment at will is established in 49 of the 50 states either by case law or statute. This default rule regarding termination of employment distinguishes the U.S. from most of the rest of the world.

While the vast majority of employees in the U.S. are employees at will, enjoying no security against termination, not all are. First, some employees have individual employment contracts that provide definite duration and good cause protection, such as many elementary and secondary school teachers who have contracts for an academic year. Second, employees represented by a union that has negotiated a collective bargaining agreement usually will have good cause protection under the collective agreement. Third, some public employees at the federal, state, and local levels work in civil service systems that, by statute, provide some form of employment security.

Although individual terminations are largely unregulated by federal law, Congress enacted a law in 1988 that regulates collective terminations—plant closures and mass layoffs. The Worker Adjustment and Retraining Notification Act ("WARN Act"), which covers employers with 100 or more employees, generally provides that employees or their union and local government officials must be given 60 days' advance written notice of a plant closure or mass layoff.

Mass layoff is defined based on number of workers or percentage of workers laid off. The penalty is payment of wages and benefits for number of days the required notice was not given. A few states have enacted their own versions of the federal WARN Act.

3. UNIONS AND COLLECTIVE BARGAINING

The current National Labor Relations Act ("NLRA") was passed in original form as the Wagner Act in 1935 and has been amended several times. Section 7, the "heart" of the Act, protects the rights of employees to "self-organization, to form, join, or assist labor organizations, to bargain collectively through representatives of their own choosing, and to engage in other concerted activities for the purpose of collective bargaining or other mutual aid or protection" and the rights of employees to refrain from engaging in any of those activities. Unlike individual employment rights law, the NLRA protects the right of employees to act collectively, using their (and their collective bargaining representative's) power to obtain from the employer whatever terms and conditions they can in a collective bargaining agreement. Thus, the NLRA does not mandate that employers provide specific minimum terms, but only protects the right of employees to collectively pursue what they can obtain. The NLRA protects the right of employees to strike, although employers may hire replacements for strikers. Whether employers are permitted to hire permanent replacements or only temporary replacements depends on whether the strike is characterized as an unfair labor practice strike or an economic strike.

Many in the U.S. do not realize that Section 7 of the NLRA protects not only employees represented by unions or seeking union representation, but also nonunionized employees who, through collective action, try to influence their working conditions. For example, employees who protest their compensation or safety conditions and seek change may be engaged in "concerted activity for mutual aid or protection," which the NLRA protects. To terminate such employees or take other adverse actions against them would be an unfair labor practice in violation of the NLRA.

The NLRA is administered by the National Labor Relations Board (NLRB), a federal agency, which has regional offices in major cities. The NLRB consists of five members, one designated as chairman, appointed by the President. The NLRB has jurisdiction over two types of cases under the NLRA: (1) representation cases—conducting elections in which employees in an appropriate bargaining unit vote on whether they wish to be represented by a union in collective bargaining; and (2) charge cases—deciding unfair labor practice charges. Both functions are performed first at the level of the regional offices by regional directors in representation cases and administrative law judges in charge cases. Decisions of the regional offices may be appealed to the NLRB. Decisions of the NLRB on unfair labor practices may be appealed to the federal courts of appeal, but representation cases cannot be appealed to the federal courts.

4. LABOR STANDARDS: WAGES, HOURS, AND BENEFITS

In many nations' labor law regimes, wages, hours, and benefits are determined principally through collective bargaining. Although collective bargaining and collective agreements can set these terms and conditions of employment in the United States, this is not the main method because the percentage of the U.S. workforce represented by unions is small. Thus, to the extent that terms and conditions of employment are regulated at all, for most employees the regulation is in the form of federal and state individual employment rights law.

Among the federal laws implicated are the following: (1) the Fair Labor Standards Act ("FLSA") (regulating minimum wage, overtime compensation, and child labor); (2) the Family and Medical Leave Act ("FMLA") (mandating leave for certain purposes); (3) the Employee Retirement Income Security Act ("ERISA") (governing pension, health, and welfare plans); (4) the Occupational Safety and Health Act ("OSH Act") (regulating conditions in workplaces that pose health and safety risks); and (5) the Consolidated Omnibus Budget Reconciliation Act ("COBRA") (extending employer-provided health insurance coverage beyond separation from employment).

The states, with considerable pressure and incentive from the federal government, passed laws to regulate workers' compensation benefits for work-related accidents and illnesses and laws to regulate unemployment insurance benefits. Many states also have passed wage payment laws that apply to aspects of wages beyond minimum wage and overtime compensation, such as how often employees must be paid. Some state and local governments also have passed laws or ordinances establishing a minimum wage that is higher than the federal minimum wage.

5. EMPLOYMENT ANTIDISCRIMINATION

One of the largest bodies of law and most active areas of employment litigation in the United States is antidiscrimination law. Federal employment antidiscrimination law in the United States prohibits adverse employment actions because of race, color, sex, religion, and national origin (Title VII of the Civil Rights Act of 1964), age (the Age Discrimination in Employment Act of 1967), disabilities (the Americans with Disabilities Act of 1990), and genetic information and testing (Genetic Information Nondiscrimination Act of 2008). Section 1981 (42 U.S.C. § 1981), a post-Civil War Reconstruction era statute, has been applied in the employment context to prohibit discrimination based on race.

Most states also have employment antidiscrimination statutes that protect the same characteristics as federal law, and some cover other characteristics, such as sexual orientation and marital status. Many local governments also have employment antidiscrimination laws.

Although Title VII also prohibits discrimination based on sex, religion, national origin, and color, the impetus behind Title VII was elimination of race-based discrimination. This is because the

United States has a history of slavery and discrimination against African Americans.

The Equal Employment Opportunity Commission (EEOC) is the federal agency charged with interpretation and enforcement of the federal antidiscrimination laws. Many states have parallel fair employment practice agencies. While many claims of discrimination are resolved by the EEOC or state agencies after the filing of charges, cases that are not resolved at the agency level may be litigated in the federal or state courts.

There are two principal theories of discrimination, which are recognized under Title VII, the ADEA, and the ADA: disparate treatment and disparate impact. Disparate treatment claims are intentional discrimination claims in which the claimant must prove that the protected characteristic was the cause of the employer's adverse employment action. Proof of discriminatory motive is crucial to a disparate treatment claim. For example, in a disparate treatment sex discrimination claim in which a woman is not selected for promotion and a man is, the claimant attempts to prove through direct and circumstantial evidence that the employer did not choose the claimant because she was female. In contrast, a disparate impact claim involves proof that a facially neutral practice or criterion has a statistically significant different effect on members of a group with a protected characteristic, and use of that practice or criterion that has such a discriminatory effect cannot be justified by business necessity. For example, if an employer makes promotions based on standardized test scores, and it is proven that African Americans perform significantly less well than Caucasians on that test, the employer may lose a disparate impact claim unless it can justify its use of the test as a business necessity.

One subset of intentional discrimination claims is harassment claims. Harassment claims often differ from other disparate treatment cases because they involve bad treatment of an employee because of her sex, race, age, disability, etc. rather than a discrete adverse employment action, such as termination or refusal to promote. Harassment is a recognized theory under all of the characteristics protected by federal employment discrimination law. Most of the principles governing the theory of harassment have developed in the cases on sexual harassment, in which the largest number of cases have been litigated.

6. PRIVACY

Privacy is a broad topic, which in the employment context can include video and audio surveillance; computer, e-mail, and Internet monitoring; drug testing; psychological testing; controlling nonworking time and activities; administering lie detector tests; probing into personal and confidential information.

Public sector (governmental) employees have greater privacy protections than private sector employees because of the U.S. Constitution and state constitutions.

There are also federal laws on privacy issues. For example, the Employee Polygraph Protection Act so severely circumscribes employers' use of lie detector tests and information obtained from their administration that employers are well advised not to give or rely on polygraphs and other lie detectors. The so-called federal Wiretapping Act of the Omnibus Crime Control and Safe Streets Act of 1968 restricts the interception of telephone calls and other communications, but it is limited in its application, and it has significant exceptions. The 1986 amendments to the Wiretapping Act, the Electronic Communications Privacy Act and the Stored Communications Act, expanded the scope of the original Act. However, these laws were not enacted with Internet-based communication in mind, and have not been a very successful tool for employees asserting privacy rights in the workplace.

There also are numerous state statutes that involve privacy issues. For example, New York, Colorado, and some other states have laws that prohibit employers from taking adverse actions against employees for engaging in lawful off-duty activities.